STAYING CONNECTED TO YOUR PARTNER

STAYING CONNECTED TO YOUR PARTNER

HOW TO OVERCOME FEAR OR UNCERTAINTY IN THE WAY YOU LOVE AND COMMIT

BARBARA T. KREEDMAN, PH.D

BK PUBLISHING

Acknowledgments

I am enormously grateful to my editor, Rick Benzel, who takes my clinical thoughts and feelings and finds a way to beautifully express them in the written word. I also want to thank Ellen Goodwin whose cover and book design are bringing this book to life. Finally, I want to thank my partner, Jack Gagne, for continued love and support throughout the writing of this book.

Other Books by Barbara T. Kreedman, Ph.D.

Why Love Stops, How Love Stays
An Interactive Workbook to Make Your Relationship Last

BK Publishing
73-725 El Paseo, Suite 23-D
Palm Desert, CA 92260
760-340-1114

ISBN: 0-9714424-1-X
10 9 8 7 6 5 4 3 2 1

TO MY PARENTS

Dad, although you are no longer here, I will carry your gift of love and support with me forever.

Mom, I learned over the years how wise you are and I am grateful to have your continuing love and support.

CONTENTS

CHAPTER I

DANCING AROUND CLOSENESS

❖ Do you go in and out of relationships? Do you feel as if you keep finding the wrong person, or continue to find fault with the person you're with?

❖ Do you want to fall in love, yet find yourself still single?

❖ Are you having difficulty making the relationship or marriage you are in work?

❖ Do you feel that your partner is stifling you or not meeting your emotional needs at all?

If any of these questions resonates with you, you are probably having difficulty with "attachment" issues. Psychologically speaking, this means that you have trouble finding and maintaining the right level of closeness with your spouse, partner, or lover. You either want more attachment than your partner gives you, or you recoil from attachment when your partner wants more closeness than you are willing to give.

Attachment issues are at the root of many relationship conflicts. I have seen this over and over again in my work as a psychotherapist for more than twenty-five years, helping singles and couples understand the "dance of closeness" they perform every day with their partner or spouse.

In most cases, relationship problems center around one of three attachment problems: one partner needs either too much attachment (referred to as dependency), or too little attachment (referred to as push-pull), or the person floats back and forth between the two feelings (referred to as wavering.) Much of the focus of my work as a psychotherapist is in helping people understand just which of these patterns they follow and why, so they can arrive at a true transformation in how they approach love and romance.

In this book, I want to offer you the same approach I use in my private practice. I know that there are dozens of relationship books on the market, offering a wide range of advice about how to fix a broken marriage or how to find a mate if you are single.

This book is different though. The work I will do with you is based on looking into the root causes of your behavior so you can get quickly to the core of your intimacy problems and truly understand your attachment issues to stop the dance you do with your spouse or partner.

If you are single and dating, wishing to find a mate, you will get insight into why you may keep going from one person to another, always thinking there is something wrong with each one or never being able to attach to the right one. If you are married and often feel unhappy with your partner (or your partner feels unhappy with you) or you are thinking about divorce, you will understand what might lie behind your dissatisfaction and why your relationship may suffer from turmoil. Whatever your situation, I will provide you with both the knowledge to understand your background better and the tools to change your behavior so you can create a healthy, loving relationship.

After reading this book, you will learn as much about yourself as my clients who work personally with me in my office. You will walk away from this book knowing why you do what you do in your relationships, and the steps to take in order to create lasting happiness.

If you currently have someone you are dating that you might be serious about, or if you are married, you may wish to have your mate or spouse read this book too. Relationships involve two people, so fixing your problems obviously works best if both of you attempt to understand your roles in creating a relationship breakdown.

Finally, let me add one important point. If you are reading this book while believing that your partner is "at fault" for all your problems, you won't make much progress. Trust me when I ask you to accept right now that both of you play a role in your intimacy breakdown, no matter what you think happens on the surface of your arguments or conflicts. Don't read this book in an effort to "fix" your partner whom you want to blame.

You need to focus in this book on getting an understanding of how your own behaviors and attitudes towards attachment play a role in your relationship conflicts. Then, if you can change yourself, you will become stronger and more able to recognize how you and your partner can resolve the problems between you. You may be able to successfully fix your relationship, but you may also realize that this is indeed the wrong person for you. At least, you will be ready to move on though, knowing much more about yourself and the type of person you may want to be with.

WHAT LIES AT THE ROOT OF MOST RELATIONSHIPS PROBLEMS

When most people first start examining their relationship difficulties in therapy, they usually focus on the wrong issues. For example, if they are constantly squabbling with their mate, they tend to go over and over in their mind what each person said and what each did. They think that by analyzing the details of their arguments and pinpointing one person to accept blame (usually their partner!), they can stop the arguing.

Or if they are constantly dating, always finding fault with people they meet, they may believe that no one can "make" them happy. They conclude that it is always the other person who is wrong or has some type of problem that interferes with the relationship.

This type of analysis is useful, but it fails to go deep enough to solve most relationship problems. Placing blame, focusing on the details of arguments, and finding faults in others is what I call surface or content therapy, which goes only skin deep and does not get to the level of true psychological understanding.

The truth is, your relationship woes reflect much deeper personality traits that may extend all the way back to your early conditioning as an infant. Believe it or not, the type of romantic bonds you form today are the result of how you learned to bond with your parents and family when you were a child. Your early environmental influences literally dictate how you attach to people today, how safe you feel in relationships, and how open you are to accepting love from others.

(**Note:** *Your life circumstances can also play a significant role in how you attach to others. However, for the purpose of this book, our focus will be solely on the developmental contribution of attachment.*)

If you are like most people who come to see me, you are probably surprised by this concept. How can my early childhood years, you may be wondering, have anything to do with my current problems with my spouse or lover? How can something that happened to me when I was two or three years old influence the fact that my spouse and I don't get along, or that I keep dating the "wrong" people? And besides, how can I go back and fix my childhood when there was nothing wrong with it or I simply can't remember it? Isn't that simply moot?

These are the types of questions that usually pop up when I talk to my clients about the early conditioning aspects of their personality development. But, if you think about it, your early conditioning clearly created the underpinnings of your personality. Even if you are not aware of it now, your early childhood became the "lens" through which you see your entire world today, including your present relationships.

There are two key psychological processes that began in early childhood and that continued throughout your adolescence and into adulthood that have shaped your attitudes towards attachment and intimacy. Understanding these two issues is the beginning of true insight into yourself and your relationships. When I work with my clients, I focus largely on these two issues. Let me give you an overview of each one, and then we will explore them in depth in the rest of the book.

FROM CHILD TO ADULT LOVER, YOU REPLAY THE SAME PATTERN!

The first psychological process that affects your ability to have a healthy, loving relationship goes back to your very earliest years. This process is called separation-individuation, referring to the time when you separated from your primary caretaker – usually your mother. Separation usually begins during infancy and reaches its peak at 36 months of life.

What happened during the separation phase is critical to your sense of self and your attitudes towards love and bonding today. As you separated from your mother, father, and/or caretaker, you received many verbal and nonverbal messages regarding your caretaker's ability to handle your emotional and physical movement away. You were made to feel good or bad, right or wrong, and safe or unsafe when you began to explore your surrounding world. These positive or negative messages became embedded in your unconscious mind, and you have carried them with you throughout your life until now.

(**Note:** *When I refer to messages that you received earlier in life, I mean verbal, nonverbal, and physical responses conveyed from the parent/and or caretaker to the infant/child. In the following discussions, the word mother is a universal reference for your primary caretaker, but it does not exclude the influence of your father or significant others in your early childhood.*)

Your separation-individuation experience was your first attachment experience. It now lies at the foundation for one of four fundamental approaches to intimacy you may have as an adult. We often call these fundamental approaches "archetypes" because they are largely true for all people. You probably fall into one of the following four archetypes:

❖ **Balanced Child → Healthy Adult Lover** – This archetype happens if your mother or primary caretaker allowed you to explore and separate without making you feel like you would lose her love. As a result, you were able to develop a healthy sense of separation. Now, as an adult, you are able to commit to a relationship without feeling that your true Self is being threatened or manipulated.

❖ **Dependent Child → Dependent Adult Lover** – Dependency arises if two conditions happened during separation. First, your mother gave you messages that it was not safe for you to physically or emotionally move away. Second, because of those messages, you feared that you would lose her love if you went against her wishes. Your fear over losing her love then created in you a tendency to abandon your own needs so that you could continue to receive the love and consistency that made you feel safe. If you received this type of early conditioning, it usually continues to impact your adulthood, in that you unconsciously continue to give up your needs in favor of pleasing others in your life, including your spouse or mate.

The complication is that, as an adult, your inner self was never really formed, and thus you never learned to identify what your needs were, let alone have them met. Yet because you continue to equate wanting something for yourself with the loss of love, you continue to have ongoing feelings of dependency.

❖ **Independent Child → "Push / Pull" Adult Lover** – This behavior occurs when your mother or primary caretaker gave you messages that it was not safe to move away, but rather than fearing the loss of love, you were unwilling to give up your natural desires. Instead, you became an independent and/or defiant infant/child. As you grew older, your independent and rebellious nature was clearly visible. You generally remained aloof from family events, participating more outside the family unit, or you rebelled against family rules and were considered the "black sheep" of the family. Today you may now exhibit what I refer to as a "push-pull" personality in that you form relationships with people, including intimate ones, but then you withdraw from them and/or create conflict with them when you consciously or unconsciously feel you will lose your sense of Self, just as you feared in your earlier years. Essentially, you constantly perform a dance of intimacy, attracting and pulling in a partner, but then through your words and actions, defying and pushing him or her away to protect the survival of your Self.

❖ **Wavering Child → Wavering Adult Lover** – This archetype happens if your mother or primary caretaker gave you mixed messages about separating. Now as an adult, you are willing to sometimes risk owning your feelings, but other times, you remain silent and aloof. At times, you can emotionally show up for your partner without fearing the consequences of loss of love, punishment, or abandonment, while at other times, you are dependent and afraid of intimacy.

While these four archetypes may seem to over-simplify intimacy problems, they are the critical underpinnings in the early formation of personality and sense of attachment with others. Your parent's approach to the separation-individuation time in your life created a profound impact on your unconscious mind, and remains ingrained in your psyche today, determining much of your adult reactions of the world.

TRANSFERENCE: WHY YOUR MATE SEEMS TO TRIGGER YOU

The second psychological process that greatly affects your ability to maintain an emotionally healthy and stable relationship is called transference. Transference refers to the fact that, throughout our lives, we all tend to interpret and react to words and situations exactly as we did from our childhood conditioning. It doesn't matter that, as adults, we have many other interpretations and emotional reactions available to us.

For example, if you were frequently yelled at by your parents, and made to feel wrong, you would have a tendency to interpret even minutely negative comments from others as if they are scolding you or correcting you just like your parents once did. If your parents often left you alone, you may have a tendency to perceive others as abandoning you or not fulfilling your needs, just as you might have interpreted your parents' reason for not being around for you. Whatever the trigger, you unconsciously recreate feelings from your childhood and transfer your old interpretations to the current moment, *causing you to misinterpret the present situation and inappropriately respond.*

Think about a recent conflict you had with your spouse or lover. Can you identify any element of that conflict in which you reacted out of transference from your past? Did your spouse or lover "trigger" a hurt or upset in you that you can trace back to a feeling that your parents gave you?

When I ask this question with my clients, most of them come to recognize at least one trigger they bring into their adult relationships from their childhood that frequently creeps into their relationship.

Like the psychological residue of separation-individuation, transference is a powerful unconscious process that interferes with your ability to maintain a healthy connection to your spouse or lover. Unless you identify and keep in check your transferences, you can easily get stuck in a "blame game," in which you believe that all conflict arises from your mate or date. But as I've said, a relationship requires two people, and each one contributes to the relationship problems in the sense that each one brings their psychological baggage to the table. You both need to understand the role that your baggage plays.

Your Early Personality Formation Is Still With You

It may still seem unbelievable that these two early conditioning processes are at the root of the behaviors and attitudes you carry into your relationships with others today. Yet once you accept how they color your view of the attachment and intimacy, how they influence the type of lover you seek out, and how they affect the quality of your interactions with people, you can begin to make progress in understanding and resolving the relationship problems you have.

So, whether you keep going from relationship to relationship, or you constantly have affairs, or you continue to find fault with your partner, or you are a workaholic who is too preoccupied to be emotionally and physically available for your mate, or you can't seem to commit to someone you love, or you keep pulling back from getting married, or you constantly argue with your spouse, or you create situations that distance you from your partner – all these relationship problems most likely stem from these two psychological keys to your personality.

The rest of this book will help you understand these two psychological processes. I intend to show you how to explore your personality archetype and identify what patterns you exhibit so that you can increase your understanding of your own unconscious approach to attachment and how it plays a part in your relationships. The more you understand about the origins and behavioral characteristics of your personality, the better equipped you will be in solving your relationship and intimacy problems.

You will also gain a better understanding of your spouse or mate's personality dynamics, even if you don't know much about his or her early childhood environment. In fact, in most cases, my approach helps each partner identify and understand how their own early conditioning plays into their partner's early conditioning.

I will also show you how to recognize where transference affects your life. The more you can recognize your own transferences, the better you will be at stopping miscommunication, arguing, and emotional disharmony between you and your mate. Recognizing transference can go a long way to cutting out conflicts and arguments in your relationship, allowing you and your partner to resolve hurt feelings much more quickly. By recognizing transferences, you can quickly know that you are acting out something from your past conditioning rather than dealing with your mate from your adult Self.

How to Use This Book

This book teaches you both concepts and practical skills. My goal is to give you a deep awareness of your own personal dynamics along with specific strategies and tools to use to improve your relationships.

In Chapter 2, we will look at the separation-individuation process, exploring in greater depth this area of personality formation. You will get a clear picture of the dilemma that all children experience: wanting continued love from your caretaker yet at the same time, needing to establish your unique Self. As long ago as this event may be from your life now, and as impossible it is to change whatever happened in your earliest years, it is nevertheless valuable to understand the impact of your separation years on your personality. Your childhood separation process influenced whether you now tend toward a dependent personality, a distant push-pull personality, or whether you have been able to achieve a healthy balance between preserving your Self and committing to others.

Chapter 2 also looks further into transference, whereby you continue to unconsciously interpret events and people in your life in the same way as you did as an infant or child. Separation and transference are highly intertwined, so your awareness of these two important psychological principles goes a long way toward analyzing your problems and taking control over unwanted reactions to others in your life.

The next three chapters are "case study" chapters. Each one contains a wide range of cases about people with whom I worked who illustrate the different personality types. Each individual client mentioned is different, and I am confident that the range of situations described will help you recognize at least a few patterns that you yourself exhibit in your own relationship. The value of case studies is that it allows you to read about the analysis and therapy I performed with each client. This can help you can gain insight and healing regarding your own issues.

In Chapter 3, you will read about some of my clients who exhibit the push-pull archetype. When push-pull people enter into a relationship or marriage, they fear becoming too attached and often believe that their partner stifles them or prevents them from having their deepest needs met. As a result, they push their partner away -- consciously or unconsciously -- by becoming workaholics or alcoholics, or by having affairs, or by acting passive-aggressively, all the while believing they are fulfilling their role in the relationship or marriage.

Chapter 4 examines the dependent archetype using an assortment of cases. This type of personality struggles with claiming his or her sense of self, frequently yielding his or her needs to others. You will read several cases that show how different dependent personality types act out their fears of losing love, such as the co-dependent person, the low self-esteem person, and the passive-aggressive dependent type.

Chapter 5 contains cases about the "wavering" personality type, which is the type of person who alternates between push-pull and dependent. Such people effectively grew up with parents who alternately gave them messages that it was both acceptable and not acceptable to move away. As a result, these people float back and forth in their relationships between being attached and being alienated from true intimacy.

Finally, in Chapter 6, I offer you a targeted program to become aware of how you are acting in your relationship due to the two psychological processes that occur in your unconscious mind. My program, called the Self-Talk Method, teaches you to monitor your behavioral patterns that influence your relationship difficulties and conflicts. As you practice the

Self-Talk method, you will begin to have control over your impulses and recognize when your own unconscious attitudes and negative behavior patterns are keeping you from establishing and maintaining a healthy, integrated relationship with someone you love.

This psychological work takes great effort. I want you to be open, honest and objective with yourself, while still being gentle and patient as you explore your childhood and early conditioning patterns. Our goal is not to encourage you to find fault with your parents for what you feel "they did to you." Nor do I want you to be too hard on yourself for your relationship problems. Right now, keep your focus on understanding the origins of your behaviors as they reflect your early childhood years so you can become aware of all the unconscious conditioned patterns and take control over behaviors that continue to dominate your life.

You may not be able to fully break out of whichever archetype you have grown up to be. Even with your great understanding from this book, your deep-seated unconscious behaviors and automatic emotional reactions to people in your life, especially your most intimate partner, can reappear without control. You may not be able to completely stop yourself from behaviors that throw your relationship into turmoil. But you will be able to alter the degree to which you inappropriately react.

I am confident that this book can significantly improve your chances of slowing the dance of intimacy that you are likely performing with your romantic partner. By identifying your triggers, you can slowly become aware of and change your approach to attachment rather than letting your childhood traumas and other life experiences continue to cloud the intimacy you desire with a romantic partner. You can indeed learn to stay connected to your partner.

Note: *The Epilogue to this book is a Self-Journal where I invite you to reflect on what you learn while reading the chapters. Here, you will find numerous pages where you can jot down notes about your separation and attachment memories from infancy, childhood, adolescence, early adulthood, and adulthood. Writing down your memories can be very useful in understanding your process and making you more aware of how the material of this book applies to you.*

CHAPTER 2

THE ORIGINS OF DEPENDENCY & DISTANCE

As a psychotherapist evaluating adult relationships, my estimate is that 80% of your relationship conflicts can be traced to how you communicate your thoughts and feelings, how you receive and interpret communication from others, and how powerful you feel while interacting with others. These three adult functions relate directly back to the conditioning you experienced in childhood from the messages you received from your parents as you attempted to move away from them. Those messages have been reinforced from your parents throughout your entire childhood and adolescence, and now as an adult, they remain embedded in your psyche forever. These three functions make the difference between feeling like a happy, fulfilled adult who can be intimate with others without feeling threatened, and feeling like someone who is losing out on life.

Early childhood is critical in the formation of our sense of attachment and relationship to others because during this time, we are open, vulnerable, and in need of acceptance from our primary caretaker. The infant and young child seeks only to please the parent and to feel secure in receiving consistent love and attention. For the young child, negative messages may suggest emotional abandonment and loss of love, while positive messages reinforce the sense of self as a separate individual who is entitled to fulfill his or her needs.

This chapter will educate you on the role that such early conditioning plays on an unconscious level in your present relationship issues. We begin with a brief foray into child development, just enough so that you can appreciate how the psychological foundation of this powerfully critical period has the potential to blur how you experience your loved ones today. Understanding this critical early conditioning and its role in today's relationship promises to improve your emotional availability and success with relationships. (It can also help you with your current parenting issues if you are a parent right now.)

As you read the information in this chapter, keep in mind that personality development is part nature, part nurture, though modern science is still uncertain about what proportion each element shares in the mix. On one hand, it is known that your genetic makeup (nature) highly dictates much about who you are– your appearance, your physical health, your emotional makeup, your thinking style and intelligence, and many other aspects of your unique individuality. But on the other hand, it is equally true that your parenting and family environment (nurture) also play a strong role in shaping your personality, behavior, and attitudes.

Think of this analogy: Humans are born like new computers off the manufacturing floor. A certain amount of hardware is built into each newborn machine that pre-defines the type of computing it can do. Equally important though are the programmers who install the other software that determines much about the types of programs the computer will be able to run.

Your personality is like such a computer. You were born with certain hardware (your genetic makeup), but you were also programmed by your family to act and react in a certain way that has become totally natural and acceptable to you. You may not remember your early programming, and you are unconscious of its influence on your personality development, but it is there. It lies behind the normal consciousness you have of your life. This is your childhood conditioning, and it continues to operate in your psyche today, affecting your approach to everything you do – from work, to friendships, to love and relationships.

THE INDIVIDUATION-SEPARATION PROCESS

Picture yourself as a baby at birth. You know nothing, have no capabilities or skills, and depend completely on the outside world for your survival. The most important object in your world is your primary caretaker, probably your mother but it could also be your father, a sibling, or another primary caretaker. It is this person to whom you are primarily attached for most of the parenting messages that tell you that you are okay and loved.

Your mother is also usually the caregiver who provides your most primitive needs such as food, sleep, bonding, and physical protection. You exist completely in "oneness" with this primary caretaker, with no distinction between her and you.

(**Note:** *Throughout this book, we will use the term "mother" to mean whichever person had the most impact during your early years.*)

But as the days and months go by, you do not stay in oneness with your caretaker for long. The human infant naturally grows, develops, and seeks to know the outside world. At some point, you infantile mind decides to venture out.

This is the first pivotal time for you, like all infants. It usually occurs within months after birth, as the infant begins to exhibit signs of wanting to move away from its primary connection. The infant starts pointing at objects outside of mother's sphere, then wants to touch these objects, and, then the coup de grâce, he or she starts to crawl and soon walks away from mother. Little by little, the infant seeks to "individuate," meaning establish its own "Self" as separate from the caretaker.

This process, as we said, is called the "separation-individuation" stage of development. It typically starts around four months of age and gets completed by 36 months of life. In this time frame, the infant's mind is naturally growing and absorbing information about the world. The child becomes totally inquisitive, curious, and observant. Through watching, touching, crawling, tasting, eating, feeling, and talking, the child begins to mature into its own "being," distinct from the mother.

This natural separation is a requirement in life, and influences the degree to which you develop a sense of "self." No infant can stay in oneness with its mother forever. It must seek to test its own powers, to establish its own turf, and to make its own decisions.

The child moves from its earliest state of being completely merged with mother -- where there is no sense of knowing where mother ends and the child begins -- to a state where there is a beginning and end to both the mother and child. When this occurs, two separate entities exist. This is a natural and healthy process of human development, and the need to be separate exists no matter what circumstances are presented for that infant.

THE GREAT DIFFERENCES AMONG US

The separation process is not automatically accomplished in the same way for all of us. We are human, not robots, so as in all human things, multiple factors can play a role in how the infant separates from the parent. When the child begins to move away from the parent, the mother's interpretation of this movement, her own ego state, her own past conditioning, and her reaction to the child wanting to separate become significant factors in determining the child's eventual personality. Let me explain.

Consider the mother who feels so close to the child that she lives in a state of oneness with her baby. She is completely bonded to her offspring. She derives pleasure from feeding it, cuddling it, and gazing in its eyes. She has never had anyone need her like this before. She feels the need to protect her baby, and sometimes in her innocence, she can overprotect and never let go. From her point of view, the child's moving away is fraught with danger, and so she tries at first to prevent the infant from roaming.

In the best of cases, some mothers eventually realize that their infant needs to explore, and so they relinquish control for a few moments. Little by little, the encouraging mother begins to grant greater freedom to the infant to leave her protection. Over time, the mother lets the child begin to define parts of its own world.

The mother and child develop an unspoken agreement about what the child can and cannot do and how far it can go. The mother lets the infant test the waters, without discouraging words or gestures, scowling, punishment, or withdrawal of love. The infant feels safe exploring the world, knowing full well that it is loved and will be welcomed back to its mother.

However, some other mothers are not so encouraging about the separation process. They become overly worried, anxious, or fearful of their child's safety. They may become controlling, strict, or punishing, believing that the child must listen to whatever they say.

This is not to suggest that these mothers are bad. They simply react that way to their infant leaving them. But there are some others who may themselves have low self-esteem and feel that the child needs to be with them to complete their own identity as "mother."

Such mothers may explicitly forbid their children to touch new objects, talk to others, and wander away, even in their own house. Or, if they let their child have a modest degree of freedom, their permission is tainted with negative messages about the safety of moving away. These mothers unconsciously transmit their worry or their deep-seated fear of being abandoned by their child.

This is a crucial time for both mother and infant. Will the mother allow or encourage the child to separate? Will she be resistant? And whichever messages the mother conveys, how will the infant react?

The effects of this process are not trivial at all. In fact, the mother/infant dynamic in the separation-individuation process plays a key role in shaping the infant's personality. The degree to which the mother accepts and allows the child to move away and the messages she conveys to the child significantly affect the formation of the child's personality and its ability to form attachments and be intimate in later life. In general, one of four patterns occurs, as shown in the chart on page 21.

These four patterns arising from the separation-individuation process are archetypal, meaning that they represent fundamental patterns of behavior among most people. They are generalizations, but, as archetypes, they apply at a high-level to the mother/child experience and intimacy issues that develop later in life. Most of us fall broadly into one of these archetypal patterns, and our behaviors and personality are completely predictable for that archetype.

If the mother...	And the child ...	The likely result will be a...
Gives positive messages encouraging the child to separate	Individuates successfully	**Balanced child →** **Balanced adult**
Gives negative messages discouraging the child to separate	Gives in to the mother and so does not individuate fully and unconsciously maintains low self esteem over giving up Self.	**Dependent child →** **Dependent adult**
Gives negative messages discouraging the child to separate	Defies the mother and individuates to avoid smothering, while unconsciously retaining anger over being devoured and having to give up the love object.	**Push-pull child →** **Push-pull adult**
Gives mixed messages about separation	Alternately gives in and defies. Wants closeness yet fears it.	**Wavering child →** **Wavering adult**

Here's an explanation of the four patterns. As you read through these, you will likely begin to recognize patterns in your life, although you may not recall your infancy and early childhood. Even if recall isn't available to you, you can observe your current interactions and notice patterns in your behavior with others, indicating your archetype. Remember: Your current behavior is a lens to your past.

THE ENCOURAGING PARENT → SUCCESSFUL INDIVIDUATION → BALANCED ADULT

This archetype represents the best of all cases, when the mother remains loving, supportive, and encouraging of the growing infant's process. This is not to say that the mother allows whatever her child wants; she still needs to set boundaries of safety around the infant as well as appropriate parenting guidelines. But overall, this mother transmits to her child the message that it is okay to venture out into the world. This type of mother has a strong ego, and she transfers that same strength of ego to her child. This mother does not fear abandonment; she knows that her infant loves her and will return safely, having indulged his curiosity for learning.

As a result of this type of early conditioning, the infant experiences a strong endorsement of its Self. The mother's encouragement and love reinforce the child's curiosity, willingness to try new things, confidence, and independence – four ingredients that make for a healthy personality and the ability to maintain strong attachments without conflict.

Barring some later traumatic event in life, this infant will move out into the world, proud of its identity and with a strong sense of Self. Most importantly, this child will mature into an adult who can have loving relationships and attachments with others. He or she will desire a healthy bond with a partner, and will be able to give and receive love without feeling threatened. He or she will likely be expressive, communicative, and supportive of the partner. People who come close to this archetype are capable of maintaining close loving intimacy without the threat of loss of self when giving to their loved ones.

Needless to say, this archetype is the paragon of the perfect mate or lover. Unfortunately, there are no perfect lovers around, because most of us grew up with less-than-perfect conditioning. Our parents were people too, and as such, they too had their own environment to deal with, creating their own unresolved material that was carried down from their own childhood into their roles as parents. Their own dynamics were bound to influence how they parented you, just as your dynamics are going to influence how you parent your children.

THE DISCOURAGING PARENT → OBEDIENT INFANT → DEPENDENT ADULT

In contrast to the above scenario is the mother who transmits to her child either conscious or unconscious messages that it is not okay to move away. Such a mother may fear for her child's safety, and so she becomes overly controlling about where her child goes. She may put the child in a metaphorical "box" in the sense that she expects the infant's behavior to fit within certain narrow limits. Or the mother may feel abandoned whenever her child leaves because her own ego is threatened as the child moves away, and so she becomes resentful, rejecting, angry, or silent.

Whatever the mother's motivation, she creates a powerful effect on the child from this type of controlling maternal feedback about the separation process. The child ends up believing that its natural inclination to separate is wrong. The child effectively translates the mother's negative feedback into an internal message along the lines of "She does not want me to do this, I must be bad." This creates a dilemma for the child.

You should also be aware that siblings can be another influence as to how the child feels about separating. If the child observes a sibling getting in trouble for wanting to move outside of the parent's wishes, it usually decides not to separate hoping to avoid the same sense of being "bad" that the infant sees in the sibling. Conversely if the child observes a sibling giving in to everything the parent wants, the child may decide not to give in and loose its own identity like its sibling. Such a child can end up taking a more rebellious path, yet feel shame, guilt, and confusion over doing so.

Ultimately, a child in this circumstance must make a choice: to obey the mother or not. This is a harsh dilemma for an infant, one that has serious repercussions on its psyche. On one hand, to obey the mother means giving up its natural human drive to be true to its Self, by separating from the mother to explore the larger world. On the other hand, not obeying — going out into the world — means risking the loss of mother's love, or so the child fears.

The choice in the young child's unconscious mind is black and white: "If I obey mother, she will love me. If I do not obey her, she will not love me." The unconscious question for the child is, do I give up myself to maintain the love from my primary love object or do I give up the love object to maintain a sense of Self.

This second archetype thus results from the child who decides to obey the mother. The obedient infant gives up some degree of its natural drive to individuate. This is not to say that the infant never separates, but rather that for this child, the process is riddled with strong messages from the mother that her needs come first. For this child, each time he or she tries to go away and the mother disapproves, the child receives a negative conditioning. Over time, this becomes increasingly ingrained in his or her mind. Slowly the conditioning shapes the infant's unconscious mind, which believes that separation is not acceptable and that his or her needs are not to be pursued.

More often than not, this type of infant will mature into a

toddler and youngster seeking the safety and comfort of the mother. Rather than risking losing mother's love, this infant will continually feel a need to "depend on" the mother for approval of its actions. This is the type of child who, at two year's old, may cling excessively to parents, will not try new activities, becomes shy and introverted, and may not socialize well with other children.

As life goes on for this child, this early conditioning often translates into an ongoing dependency on other people for validation of his or her identity. In the latency period of development (ages 8 to 12), the child may be reserved and shy, have difficulty socializing, possibly not be capable of having overnights with other children, being homesick, and so on. Later, as a teen, this person may experience further loss of self-esteem, confidence, and asserting his or her own wants. He or she may fall into the wrong crowd, becoming a follower to a strong leader whose approval he or she seeks to unconsciously mimic the approval he or she received from the parent at the earlier age.

For most dependent children, barring intervention or another life trauma, they may grow up to become adults who form submissive relationships, giving up their needs in favor of their partner's desires. You can recognize a dependency dynamic in people who stay in an unloving relationship or feel powerless to direct their relationship. They blame their partner over decision-making issues, yet they themselves refuse to stand up for their own rights due to fear of repercussions (i.e., the loss of love). They may tolerate inappropriateness from their partner and give in during the early years of marriage.

Sometimes with such people, after years of marriage and/or the feeling that life is passing them by, their unresolved separation issues may suddenly rear up in adulthood, causing them to crave the fulfillment of their own needs. You probably know someone like this (or it may be you), who suddenly rebels against the spouse and sets out to live the type of life they have always desired. As a dependent person, they have tended to live their life through their spouse or their children, but now they desire to strongly define their own life. Their choice to be dependent stopped working for them as they now realize how unfulfilled they are, and they are no longer willing to live through others. They now want to fulfill their needs and take life into their own hands.

Note: Another scenario behind dependency may not come from the mother but from the father. As the child develops, the father may be a strict disciplinarian verbally or physically, and not allow the child to go in the direction it desires. Instead, this type of father keeps a tight rope on the wants, interests, outside activities, sports and education of the child. The child must obey the predetermined outline as set forth by the father, or risk total disapproval. The child succumbs to the wants of the father and becomes his mirror image, or perhaps what the father could not himself ever accomplish. As an adult, this type of dependent person resents the life that they never planned out for themselves and are susceptible to drug or alcohol abuse to numb the anger within.

THE DISCOURAGING PARENT → DEFIANT INFANT → PUSH-PULL ADULT

This archetype also involves a mother who transmits the message that separation is not okay. However, in contrast to the infant who capitulates to the mother's conscious or unconscious messages, this child defies the parent to some degree, insisting on being true to its inner Self to explore the world. For this type of child, the risk of losing its true Self is far greater than the risk of losing maternal love. This is not to suggest that this child never needs maternal love, but rather that this type of infant does not yield its natural curiosity to move away from mother.

Such a mother/child struggle often results in what is called a "push-pull" dynamic. On one hand, the infant naturally seeks its mother's attention whenever it feels the need for love; the child "pulls" in love just as any infant does. But on the other hand, this infant does not want to abandon its true Self; it needs to control when to be separate and when to come back to mother's safety.

For this child, maternal love sometimes feels threatening and smothering, and so it emotionally flees from its mother. As a result, this child "pushes" the love object away whenever it gets too close for comfort. In the end, this child becomes conditioned to a pendulum-like emotional swing, alternately pushing and pulling on love.

You can recognize the push-pull dynamic going on when you see a toddler running from a mother's hugs, or grimacing with dislike over being smooched, or refusing to answer when he is busy in play. In these moments, the toddler is essentially replying to the maternal expression of attention, love, or obedience with a resounding, "No, I'm in control here."

When these children burst out in their adolescent years, they may become highly vociferous rebels, aiming to maintain control of their lives away from what they perceive as a domineering parent. In some cases, these rebelling teens become attracted to violence or crime, slipping across to the other side of the spectrum as they try to shed their dependency. In most cases, the teen excludes the parent in every way from knowing anything about their world. They dislike their controlling parent but cannot find a harmonious way to assert themselves without detaching completely. Their rebelliousness represents the black/white manner in which they see the world — it's their way or my way.

Barring other life trauma or intervention, the push-pull child who becomes highly conditioned to this dynamic will mature into a push-pull adult, living the same emotional pendulum swings when it comes to love and intimacy. These adults express their push-pull tendencies in a variety of behaviors, ranging from refusing to commit to a monogamous relationship, to getting married but never truly settling down or being loyal to their partner, to becoming workaholics which allows them to avoid intimacy, to using some form of substance abuse to avoid intimacy.

Many push-pull adults unconsciously set up roadblocks to prevent their partner from getting too close. I often compare this to creating a "moat" around themselves to protect themselves from their ultimate enemy: their sense that another person is smothering or dominating them, leading to the loss of their Self. These adults literally create turmoil and conflict as a means of staving off too much closeness that reminds them of their overly domineering parent. They see actions of love and intimacy as a threat to their survival. Loving gestures and need for closeness are experienced as intrusions and forms of domination.

THE WAVERING PARENT → WAVERING CHILD → WAVERING ADULT

This last archetype is a merger of the two types of early conditioning discussed above. The wavering personality is actually the most common pattern I see in my office. Experiencing both the push-pull and dependency archetypes, this type of person alternatively gives in or rebels, wavering between the two extremes in adult relationships. The wavering personality is the product of a mother or caretaker who gave her child mixed signals about separating, alternating between positive and negative messages in some way. Such parents may outwardly encourage their infant to move away, but upon seeing the child take too much control, they react and pull the child back. The infant is then confused, thinking that the parent had first endorsed the move away, but then believing that their interpretation must have been wrong.

You can recognize the wavering child when you see a toddler who refuses to voice his opinion or needs, or who says one thing and does another. Behind such a toddler is a parent who is sending mixed signals to the child.

As the wavering toddler grows into latency and adolescence, he or she may become the type of person who cannot seem to trust their own judgments and instincts. There remains for this person a lingering doubt about the world, making it hard for them to make decisions about their goals, their relationships, and their life. They may attempt many projects and activities, but frequently give up because they don't feel confident about their decisions, always anticipating negative repercussions.

Important characteristics of this archetypal personality are a lack of trust in the Self and a lack of consistency in their reactions to others. The wavering person depends heavily on outside validation, leaving them uncertain about which direction to take. Their adult relationships can never be satisfying, and their behavior reflects ongoing contradictions as they vacillate between dependency and fleeing.

As an adult, the wavering person may float from job to job, from relationship to relationship, and from marriage to marriage, never quite sure of what feelings and goals to pursue in life. They continue to drive people around them crazy because their behavior remains contradictory and inconsistent, vacillating between dependency and rebelliousness.

PHASES OF LIFE REVISITED

Understanding the separation-individuation dilemma and the early conditioning you receive from your parents and family provides extensive insight into a wide variety of developmental phases and psychological issues in an individual's life. To a large degree, this analysis actually helps you redefine or reframe many adult issues that might trouble you as an individual, as a lover, and even as a parent. Consider the following areas that you can now view in a completely different light using these archetypal traits:

Redefining the Terrible Two's

You've undoubtedly heard the expression "the terrible two's," referring to the second year of an infant's life when, as is commonly said, "all hell breaks loose." During this period, most infants become highly prone to stubbornness, rebelliousness, and outright nastiness. When they do not get their way, they whine, kick, scream, cry, and just plain disobey their parents.

What should be clear to you now is that the terrible two's are essentially the first major explosion of the separation-individuation process. Two-year-olds are reacting to the messages from parents that might be encouraging, discouraging, or confusing them. Especially if the parent is dominant, punishing, strict, or demanding that the child's behavior stay within certain limits, the attempt at controlling the infant effectively thwarts its natural curiosity. All children want to test their powers in some fashion.

But as you've read in this chapter, the degree to which the child wants to venture out AND the degree to which they are parentally-controlled determine whether they become a healthy, dependent, push-pull, or wavering child -- and by extension, whether as adults they will have difficulties being close, staying close, and making commitments.

Redefining Teenage Rebelliousness

Being two years old is not the only time in human development when rebelliousness arises. If you recall your own teen years -- or you have a teenager right now -- you know that teens test the waters of parental authority nearly every day. Perhaps you can now understand that, happening behind the scenes during the teen years, is essentially another major explosion of the separation-individuation process.

As suggested in the descriptions above, there is a major disruption during the teen years. The dependent child may stay on track, or for the first time become a defying teen with self-esteem and confidence problems stemming from the early conditioning by a dominating parent. The child has exposure to other teens and sees what they are allowed to do. The dependent child is given permission from outside to change the rules. The closeness between parent and child that prevailed all these years now becomes threatened. It is as if a new child has surfaced, one that you might feel you have never known.

In actuality, however, the child is still the loving child you have always known but now wants more of a voice, yet doesn't know the right way to go about it. This rebelliousness can be easily altered if the parents are willing to hear their new young adult, rather than continuing to control and force the child to remain silent and obedient. The parents need to see that their child still needs to be parented, just in a different way.

Meanwhile, the push-pull child usually becomes a push-pull teen, continually trying to commit to life but feeling smothered from time and time and so rebelling to avoid parental attachment. And the wavering child still wavers, unsure if making his or her mark on the world will create a loss of love from significant others.

Each of these archetypes struggles with their identity and self-image during the teen years. In addition, teens are more exposed to social and peer group pressures, and they usually gain the wherewithal (such as a phone, Internet, private room, car, etc.) to be more independent and mature. Given these two forces, the teen years can become a time for a person to remake themselves to some extent, effectively saying to parents, "I will now do it my way, and I have the wherewithal to do it too."

Unfortunately, as we said earlier, some teens make bad choices here, going too far to the other side of the spectrum and getting involved in drugs, sex, crime, or violence, as they rebel against their parents and their own self-image. The dependent child may transfer his dependence from the parent to a popular school figure or may substitute in place of the parent a boy- or girlfriend who becomes the new object of their dependency. Meanwhile, the push-pull child, when a teen, isolates himself from family and involves himself in outside activities such as sports, drama, or even working, where freedom can be expressed and the parent lacks control over the child. And the wavering teen might become so unable to make decisions that he or she is plagued with doubt, fear, and paralysis over which direction to take.

In short, the teen years are a second explosion of the separation-individuation process, with continuing fears over what repercussions will take place when the young adult asserts itself.

Redefining Codependency

The term co-dependency has become very popular of late, coming to mean a person who unconsciously gives in even when they don't want to. In light of what we've covered in this chapter, perhaps you can see that co-dependency has roots that can be traced back to the time when the early conditioning damaged the person's sense of Self. As children, co-dependent people were given explicit or implicit messages that they were bad, that something was wrong with them for wanting their needs fulfilled outside the wants of their parents. Again, this is not to suggest that the parents were a priori horrible, mean, or bad. It only means that, as children, such people constantly interpreted their parents' messages in a way that led them to feel bad when they didn't want what their parents wanted. They resorted through their early conditioning to conforming behaviors such as constantly agreeing, giving up their wants, not speaking up, or simply withdrawing and seeking to be invisible.

Now as adults, they continue to act out their dependency, not because they want to but rather because this is all they know. Their reality is black and white -- do what it takes to remain safe, be loved, and prevent emotional abandonment at whatever cost.

Unfortunately, what complicates matters for the co-dependent person is that their partner may also be acting out his or her own psychological problems. As a couple, the two partners are like the earth and the moon, forever spinning around each other, never able to break out of their negative habits that feed upon each other. To an extent, co-dependent people know they should change, grow up, and assert themselves. If they married someone who is too controlling, they know they should alter their situation, but they simply can't. Their early conditioning messages teaching them not to individuate were so strong that even as adults in an abusive, unloving, or dissatisfying relationship, moving away is too threatening. They cannot tolerate the loss of connection and love, so once again they give up their Self to maintain a safe and sound merger with their object (the spouse or mate).

Redefining Food Disorders

Another important area for which this analysis provides a new perspective is food disorders, such as anorexia and bulimia. While these conditions may arise to some degree from teen peer group pressures to be thin, they may have deeper roots in the separation-individuation stages of early conditioning under a controlling, dominating, or fearful parent. Whereas the highly controlled young child was granted little power over his or her body and mind, the adolescent seeks to recapture that power by taking control using food. The young adult is in essence acting out regaining control by transferring the control object from "parent" to "food." The mind of this person believes that it finally has control over what it wants to do, even when the decision hurts the Self as it does with many food disorders. Their focus on weight is really an expression of self-control versus someone else having control. Although the thinking may sound distorted, the need for the young adult to finally have control over the domineering environment of the past seems to outweigh the concern over self-abuse in the present.

COMMON QUESTIONS

I hope this brief background in what developmental theorists call "object relation" theory and the separation-individuation process is already enhancing your perspective of your current relationship issues. However, some people have questions and doubts about how such early childhood conditioning could possibly still hold sway over their lives. Some of the most common questions and concerns include the following:

Q: I can't remember anything about my childhood, so how can this really influence me today?

It doesn't matter if you don't recall this period of your life. The fact is, sometime between your being 18 and 36 months of age, your parents began to condition you to a certain type of response whenever you attempted to explore, venture away, or assert yourself from your primary caretaker. Regardless of what intention your parents had, your mind interpreted their directives as negative or positive, and those messages have influenced your psyche in a very deep way. The chart below shows the phases of the separation-individuation process, indicating the powerful impact this phase has on human personality development.

Age	Name of Stage	Behavior	Normal Outcome
0-4½ mo.	*Symbiosis*	Time when mother and child are merged.	Child is autistic-like because the merger between child and parent is so complete. (If the child lacks an adequate merger, this can lead to psychotic personality.)
5 mo.-18 mo.	*Refueling*	Time when child moves away from mother yet returns to get love.	Beginning stages of separation. The child alternately returns for safety and ventures out. In later life, adult comes home for security, but leaves again.
18mo-36mo.	*Rapproachment*	Child's ego stronger and begins to separate more from parent.	Child faced with 3-way choice: 1) it is okay to pull away and venture out on its own or 2) it must give up Self to maintain connection (dependency) or 3) it must give up connection to maintain Self (push-pull syndrome).
36 mo. and above	*Individuation*	Child learns to be separate from parent without fear of reprisal.	Completion of separation-individuation process. Adult feels secure within Self and with connection of others.

Q: I don't have any recollection of my parents being negative, dominant, or controlling, and they are not that way now. Is this significant?

It also doesn't matter if you don't recollect that your parents were mean, domineering, or controlling, and in all likelihood, they were not. More likely is that your parents were simply young, or overwhelmed with the demands of having a family and earning a living, or were unconsciously dealing with their own demons. Nonetheless, in most cases, you were presented with strong messages that remain intact into your adulthood and influence how you let others into your world.

Q: Didn't my parents notice what they were doing to me?

No, your mother and father were as unconscious of their behavior as you are of yours right now. They too grew up a certain way under their parents, who made them into the people they were when you were born. If your parents were controlling and dominating, your grandparents likely were too, and their effort to control your parents as young children led to a repetition of the archetype from one generation to the next.

Conversely, some parents try to present a completely different experience to their children in an effort to undo what was done to them. But this too can present its own set of problems. For example, take a mother who was controlled in her childhood and who, in an effort to undo what was done to her, now allows her children to do whatever they want. However, the children don't know that the mother is rebelling from her childhood. All the children learn is that anything goes. The problem is, life isn't like that, and once in the world, it can be a big awakening for these children. Spoiled at home means spoiled in life and when life doesn't make things easy, major adjustment problems can occur.

Again, this is all the result of the parent not wanting their child to experience what they disliked, yet the end result is that the mother has gone way too far the other way.

In short, the way a parent brings up their child will become the way that child becomes a parent herself, raising her own child.

> **Q: Whatever may have happened to me in my infancy, aren't there other events later in my life that would have taken over or moderated my early conditioning?**

Yes, there are likely many other events in life that affect you, but a person becomes predisposed through early childhood conditioning to a certain type of response. As a result, the psychological impact of many events later in your life is lost on you. You may get support for your needs from your peers in school, but for the most part, you continue to get opposing messages from your home, and you may still feel guilty inside for disobeying your parents. You thus revert back to old patterns and ignore positive messages now available to you.

> **Q: I don't feel that I am always one way or the other. For example, I think I am a very different person at my work than I am at home with my spouse. What do you say to that?**

A combination of personality styles between work and home is very common, but various elements explain this behavioral dichotomy and do not mitigate the fact that however you are at home is usually the way your are in life. For example, consider a businessperson who seems strong, independent, and aggressive but then appears weak and dependent at home. What explains this split personality is that, at work, the person has been asked, even authorized by the company, to take control and be aggressive. In addition, at work, there is likely no threat of personal abandonment; a misstep will not cause the person to lose his object of love. But at home, this same person is acting out his true dependent early conditioning because his loved one represents a far greater threat to his psyche. The loved one essentially becomes the parent object, for whom they fear of loss of love if they were to risk challenging the decisions of their spouse.

HOW TRANSFERENCE REINFORCES YOUR ARCHETYPE

So far in this chapter, you have seen how the separation-individuation process sets off the first domino in your personality development. The early years of your life, between 18 months and 3 years of age, are critical in influencing how your personality forms and what unconscious messages you absorb from your parents.

But there is another piece of the puzzle, as mentioned in Chapter 1, regarding why you may be having relationship problems today. This second element is transference, which refers to your tendency to interpret events today as if they were events from your childhood. You transfer your feelings from childhood into a current situation, which causes you to misinterpret and/or overreact to people around you.

Transference arises out of a natural psychological conditioning process and doesn't mean that there is anything wrong with you. However, it adds another layer of unconscious behavior on top of your early conditioning archetype, and the two combined can contribute to creating conflict and unhappiness in your romantic relationships.

Let me explain more specifically how transference affects your current relationship. Whenever you and your partner become intensely emotional with each other during conflicts, or you miscommunicate to the point of not being able to resolve whatever relationship problems you have, it is usually a sign that one or both of you is unconsciously feeling helpless, controlled, punished, etc. Your unconscious feeling arises from the childhood conditioning you had whenever your parents made you feel threatened or insecure.

Rather than seeing your partner in the here and now, listening to the real words said, the person in transference unconsciously reverts back to unresolved childhood feelings and mimics the behaviors from that time. The person essentially transfers the old situation onto the current one. This transference causes the person to repeat behaviors created in childhood, rather than living in the current situation. You therefore react to the situation in inappropriate ways, rather than dealing with it as an adult who has many choices.

Transferences happen because we all unconsciously hold onto emotions and experiences from our childhood, just as we do with the emotions and experiences that contributed to our personality formation from the individuation-separation process. The mind automatically stores these past events and our feelings about them. When a current situation reminds us of one of these old situations, we unconsciously replay the old feelings and thinking patterns we developed rather than acting from our adult rationale Self.

For example, you may once have been scolded by your parent for refusing to do a chore. Today, if your mate asks you to do an errand, it may unconsciously provoke in you a fear that you will be scolded again, and so you might lash out at your partner rather than answering with a simple yes or no.

Transferences are not always based on a negative childhood experience. You can also transfer positive experiences inappropriately. For instance, you may have had fond feelings for an aunt or uncle in your childhood who treated you well. In today's world, you can then end up transferring those feelings onto someone you've just met who looks or acts like that person. You automatically attribute positive qualities to the new person because he or she seems to possess the same qualities as your childhood relative.

You are probably familiar with the word "triggered." I use this word to alert my clients that they are in a transference. You can tell when you are triggered and thus in a transference when:

❖ You react in a highly emotional manner to a situation.

❖ You feel a sense of helplessness and powerlessness in dealing with a problem.

❖ You characterize a situation as "always" happening to you or a person as "never" doing what you want.

❖ You have a sense of being out of control, even slightly.

❖ You find yourself responding to your mate (or anyone) at a higher level of energy than the situation deserves.

❖ You find that you want to blame someone or something else for your actions.

❖ You lose trust in the person you're speaking with.

❖ You find yourself not listening to the person.

❖ You feel like closing down and shutting out the world.

All these are signals that you are likely in transference, and therefore not acting from your rational adult mind.

Transferences can be destructive to your relationship because, as I said, they are another layer of unconscious behaviors on top of your early conditioning archetype. Couples with relationship difficulties that stem from their transferences unknowingly suffer from communication problems because one or both of them is not truly present, listening to their partner in the moment. Instead, he or she is unconsciously reliving an experience from childhood, leading to unproductive feelings and reactions to the partner.

I have written a previous book that delves far more extensively into the subject of transference and how it affects you in your relationship. Entitled *Why Love Stops, How Love Stays*, I highly recommend that you read this other book in addition to the work you are doing here. That will help you understand the concept of transferences in depth and to determine where yours may come from. With that knowledge, you can learn how to prevent them from controlling your reactions with your partner.

Meanwhile, it is important that you also have an understanding of transferences for this book. Many of the case studies you will read in the next chapters will show you how both psychological conditioning processes – separation-individuation and transferences – can shape personality and affect your ability to maintain a healthy, loving relationship.

CHAPTER 3

THE PUSH-PULL PERSONALITY

The push-pull personality is an archetype, but it does not translate into the exact same behavior in all people. That is to say, push-pull people may act out their early childhood conditioning and their ongoing transferences in many ways, depending on other aspects of their personality, most especially their ability to be aware of their feelings and trigger points. Think of the push-pull personality as being able to have a spectrum of relationships, with some people managing to get seriously involved in a relationship and perhaps get married, while others cannot even attract a partner.

What unifies push-pullers into an archetype is that they all ultimately waiver in their ability to permanently commit and attach to a partner. At some point in each relationship they have – whether it occurs fairly early in the dating phase or after they've been married for a number of years – the push-puller struggles with staying attached to their mate.

Commitment unconsciously frightens them, makes them feel they have lost control of their life, and infringes on their sense of freedom. The push-puller may then act out these unconscious feelings by fleeing the relationship, or staying but becoming emotionally unavailable, or by seeking escape from the relationship in their work, or by using drugs, alcohol, or affairs to avoid truly committing to their partner.

This chapter portrays the wide-range of such "alternative patterns" that push-pullers live out. Based on the many clients I have worked with (but whose stories I have modified to protect their privacy), I have included five profiles that are commonly indicative of push-puller relationship problems. I have carefully described the cases to provide you with realistic and identifiable examples of relationship issues you may be facing, so that you can truly see how I work with patients and the depth of analysis it takes to understand the complex emotions involved in a relationship. You may identify with one of the patterns in this chapter as your own, or perhaps as that belonging to your partner.

Many adults with relationship problems think the reasons are simple and straightforward. They may either blame their partner for all problems, or they may resort to an "easy out" by saying the relationship or marriage was not right for them. In reading this chapter, however, I am asking you to look with me more deeply, behind the scenes, to the forces that your early childhood conditioning exerts on your life. In almost all cases, you will find that your early childhood upbringing, family environment, and adult transferences play a more critical role in your problems than you believe. Once you accept this, you will begin to truly understand how your relationship problems are caused, to some degree, by your own unresolved psychological issues, if you fit into the push-pull personality.

THE SHORT-TERMER

The short-termer refers to the type of push-puller who consistently finds relationships but bails out of them before romance has any chance of developing. Here's a case of one such individual.

Bill, a 40-year-old single male, came in to see me because he had just ended a relationship. He felt that he had "almost" found the woman of his dreams, but he suddenly called off the romance. Bill struggled to explain to me exactly what happened between his lover and him, and this made me focus on the sudden change in feelings. As we talked, he finally proclaimed that his former lover had a serious "flaw" that caused him to terminate the relationship.

People who have trouble in relationships usually follow a pattern, so I asked Bill if he often finds the exact same so-called "flaw" with any other women he had dated or if he experiences the same sudden change of feelings about each new partner. Of course, recognizing your own pattern of behavior is about as easy as seeing the end of your nose (something for you to think about!), so it was not surprising that Bill replied negatively, that he didn't believe he always found the "exact same" flaw. What he admitted though, and perhaps what prompted him to come into therapy, was that at a certain point in his dating, he always lost interest in his girlfriend. Something clicked in him that made him feel that each woman was not the "perfect match" anymore, and that he had to reject her. He then enjoyed meeting a new woman, and testing to see if she was the right woman for him.

On the surface, you might interpret Bill as simply the type of person who just innocently likes to date and date, but in reality, he is the proverbial "short-termer" push-puller. Whether a man or woman, the pattern is always the same: they seem to enjoy the chase aspect of romance, but no matter how good the relationship is, they just don't like the idea of commitment. As a result, they flee, invariably justifying themselves by claiming that their partner had some type of personality defect, seemingly valid, that was to blame for the breakup.

If this resonates with you, I suggest that you read this carefully. A continual pattern of dating ending in broken romances because of so-called "imperfect partners" usually indicates that you are enacting a push-pull behavior arising from early childhood conditioning that created an ambivalence in you toward intimacy and connection. You attempt to connect emotionally with your partners, but then your unconscious feelings about being connected make you feel like you are losing your freedom or being smothered. But rather than truly assessing your feelings for your partner, you react automatically and move away. Such unconscious motives usually arise from your early childhood conditioning, as you've been learning.

In Bill's case, his early years had just the right ingredients to create this relationship ambivalence. The baby in his family, with two older sisters, Bill recalled his childhood as being a happy one, and his family made him feel that he was truly loved. However, he recalled always feeling overly protected, being the youngest. He reported that he was frequently the center of attention in the family, which left him believing that he had to make everyone happy. As the only son, he had to play sports with his dad; as the little brother, he had to allow himself to be taken out by his sisters; and as the baby, he became the one in whom his mother confided.

Bill's environment was obviously a healthy, close loving family. But you don't need to grow up in a dysfunctional family to create the push-pull pattern in your psyche. All that matters, as you've read in the previous chapters, is whether the messages from your parents encouraged you to separate, individuate, and be your own person -- or discouraged you from doing so.

The analysis for Bill became clear. With so much attention placed on him, Bill grew up feeling that he could not please himself without feeling guilty at the same time about not pleasing those around him.

When I explained this concept to him, he recognized himself immediately. He remembered feeling that, as a child, he couldn't go off and do his own thing without thinking that some family member wanted to be with him instead. When his father came home from work, he would look forward to playing some form of sports with Bill. Mother looked forward to the late evening when she could talk to him about her day since her husband was always tired and went to bed early. And the older sisters always wanted something or other from Bill, which made him feel more overpowered than loved. In essence, Bill simply could not establish his own world when he was a child.

As an adult, Bill now has the same unconscious feelings of being pressured whenever it comes to being with others, especially a girlfriend. His conditioning of having to constantly please his family and not be able to establish his private world was carried forward into his world today, which he was unconsciously acting out. Whenever his girlfriends made him feel trapped, confined, or in some way unable to be separate and free as he wanted, he resorted to breaking off his relationships and finding faults in his girlfriends.

When I asked Bill if he understood how he did this, he smiled. He could definitely see that he always felt pressure when dating, and that his girlfriends invariably seemed to want more than he could give. In his unconscious mind, Bill's romantic partners were like his family members. Their wanting more from him was like his family's constant wanting to be with him. The only difference is that, as a child, Bill didn't want to disappoint his family, and so he could not say no. But now as an adult, he could, and so saying no became his way of asserting himself to his girlfriends.

What doesn't dawn on Bill, or any short-termer, is that adults have other ways to establish their wants without feeling guilty or disappointing someone. Rather than abandoning a potentially viable romantic partner, you can communicate and negotiate to get the space you need. You can become aware of when you might be knee-jerk reacting to your partner's reasonable needs for love and affection, rather than automatically feeling that your partner is asking too much from you.

If you have a tendency to have short-term romances, you therefore want to begin by becoming more aware of your feelings when you are with your partner. If you actually enjoy being with the person, and feel you love the person, but at the same time feel smothered by their needs to connect with you, it is likely that you are acting out an old scenario from your past rather than living out your true feelings. Learning to set boundaries without the fear of being abandoned is a key element to moving through this period.

THE "THERE BUT NOT THERE" PARTNER

This archetype is similar to the short-termer, except that rather than physically disappearing by breaking up, this person emotionally disappears from the relationship while physically staying in it.

Take John, a 45-year-old divorced male who came into therapy because he was dating a woman with whom he claimed he wanted to settle down, but at the same time, he insisted that this relationship plagued him. Notice that dichotomy of feelings John exhibits – a sure sign of a push-pull pattern.

As I questioned John for details, he explained to me that he thought he really loved his girlfriend. To exemplify how much he loved her, he said that whenever he wasn't with her, he missed her greatly and was always calling her to find out where she was and what she was doing. He thought they had great phone conversations, and he loved the sound of her voice.

But the kicker was that whenever he stayed with her for a weekend or over a long period of time, he felt stifled and wanted to escape from being with her. When I asked him if his girlfriend sensed this, he acknowledged that his inconsistent attitude drove her crazy and, of course, completely destabilized their relationship. She herself was almost ready to give up the relationship, and so the two were struggling.

I asked John about his childhood. He told me his father was very strict with him. While his younger sister didn't have problems with their dad, John was constantly getting into trouble. He recalled that he was always excited and eager to do new things and go to new places, but this created problems for his parents who found him too active. They often punished him when he went outside the perimeters of what they expected. I call this type of behavior operating outside the "box."

Little boys particularly show exuberance and a healthy desire to investigate. Upon receiving negative messages when testing their limits, the child, as well as the unresolved adult, feels resentful of limit setting as well as fearful of being controlled.

Looking back now, John understood that he was basically a good kid, but that his parents simply had expectations of him that weren't in line with his personality. We could both see that he was cordoned off by his family's rules, and was made to feel bad for wanting more. Though he never acted out his frustration at home or school through drugs or alcohol, John simply never received the freedom he wanted as a boy or young man.

The effects of John's early childhood parental messages were serious. As an adult, here was John, in a good relationship and in a position to get married. However, he was in a Catch 22 about the potentially happy prospect of being married. He loved the woman, but marriage unconsciously triggered in him a sense that he would lose his freedom, exactly just as his parents had ruled his childhood needs. In John's mind, marriage meant that he had to give something up to be with his girlfriend, to please her, and to satisfy her needs for companionship.

John's unconscious dilemma fits the pattern for many people who view their spouse or lover as controlling them. They then disappear for periods of time, making their lover feel they are "there but not there." Actually, even if you claim that your spouse or lover is truly a demanding person, it is still likely that you are reliving an early childhood conditioning that causes you to overreact to your partner.

In John's case, we had a little of both problems occurring. From his description of the situation, it did seem that his girlfriend was a woman who insisted that he constantly choose her over any of his other activities and enjoyments. For example, John enjoyed weekend sports, but she was constantly insisting that he spend his entire weekend doing things she enjoyed doing. In this way, she pushed his "autonomy button" quite often. At the same time, John did not deal with his girlfriend's needs in an honest, loving way. Rather than compromising on both their needs, he resorted to the pattern from his youth, wherein he escaped from his parent's control through sports.

As an aside, note that resorting to sports every weekend in your life is often indicative of a push-pull pattern. On the surface, playing sports seems completely healthy and fitting, but there is often an unconscious component that extends from your childhood if your parents allowed sports as the only legitimate avenue for a child to gain freedom from them. Many parents control their children within the home environment, but allow them to escape through sports, and so this form of self-expression continues into adult life for such individuals.

Back to John, once we understood the childhood origins for his mixed feelings about his potential marriage partner, my goal became to make him aware of the triggers that caused him to feel like running away from her on weekends. In this case, there was a clear trigger point. Whenever John wanted to play a sport or get time to himself in some other way, he would ask her for permission. When she occasionally agreed he could do what he wanted, things were fine between them. But whenever she said no to his request, which was the usual case, his childhood conditioning unconsciously erupted, making him feel trapped just as he had been as a kid.

In truth though, John interpreted his girlfriend in a far more threatening way than she intended. In many cases, her requests for time with him were legitimate. So if John could become aware of his early childhood conditioning, he could open himself to possible solutions.

For example, the two of them might honestly discuss their schedules, and learn to balance John's need for freedom through sports vs. her need for companionship. Or they could compromise by alternating activities on weekends, or any other negotiated settlement between them. But one thing was clear: without being aware of his early conditioning and learning to recognize when he became triggered, John would likely continue to alienate any potential mate with a lifetime of his "there but not there" behavior. This personality has an ongoing unconscious sense to not give in to the wants of others and risk the potential loss of the relationship. The compelling need to give to others needs to be balanced with satisfying the needs of the Self and at the same time not fearing an adverse response.

THE FIGHTER

The fighter is another guise taken on by push-pullers. As you might expect, the fighter is someone who constantly battles with their mate to create distance and chaos, rather than sustaining a close loving romance.

Phil, a 54-year-old man, came into therapy telling me that his family was absolutely "fed up" with him. He explained that his wife had just asked him for a separation and that his children, who were away in college, never called him at all. Phil was feeling very sad, and said that he loved his family, but he just couldn't seem to stay connected to anyone. Whenever he tried to talk with his wife or children, a battle erupted. Phil admitted that he "sometimes" had a short temper, but he claimed his anger lasted only a few minutes and then he could calm himself down. As he reflected on his family in our first session, he concluded that everyone else "just didn't understand him." (By the way, whenever you believe others don't understand you, it's usually a sign that you have felt this feeling before.)

I began to explore Phil's relationship with his current family, seeking out a pattern of behavior. Did he overreact to everything in their lives, or just some things? Phil thought about it and realized that many of the eruptions in his family centered around times when he believed that his wife or kids were requesting favors of him or telling him what to do. When he thought this, Phil felt compelled to either acquiesce to their needs or yell at them. I pointed out that he could politely say "No," but Phil replied that he thought that his family just could not tolerate the word "no" from him. Whenever he wanted to tell them no, he believed he had to raise his voice to stop them from insisting on more.

When I asked him what it feels like when he thinks he can't stop the members of his family from having their way, he replied that he felt trapped, as if he had no say and was being forced into doing something that he didn't want to do. Through our discussion, Phil realized that his reactions to his family were not just signs of random anger, but rather his anger had a message. It was his way to stop the impending sense of feeling powerless and trapped into doing what he didn't want to do, a carryover of childhood conditioning.

I asked Phil if he recalled similar feelings of feeling powerless or trapped from his childhood. He thought a bit and then had a therapeutic moment of recognition, that yes, he often felt trapped by his family when he was younger.

Here is an example of adult behavior – uncontrollable anger – that has its roots deep in someone's childhood. We probed deeper into Phil's early years. The oldest of three boys, Phil recalled that his parents always expected him to do things "right" and to be a model for his younger siblings. He grew up with a sense of pressure being put on him. When I asked him if he could ever say no to his parents, he answered that he constantly felt obligated to make his parents happy. I asked Phil if he ever "acted out" in any way during his teen years to vent his anger, such as through drinking, drugs, or getting into trouble, and he admitted that he got into a little trouble in high school, but that it was short lived. For the most part, Phil was proud of his morals and ethics, reflecting that he had always done the right things and had made his best effort to take care of others before himself.

The situation in Phil's marriage was becoming clear. Here was Phil, age 54, in a long-term marriage with children, but now as an adult, he continued to feel the pressure from his childhood to do things right. The only way that he could now say no to those around him was by using his temper. Just as he couldn't say "no" in his earlier years, his adult mind unconsciously continued to feed him the message that he needed to make everyone happy. Although Phil wouldn't have dared transgress as a child to the point where he would disappoint his parents, he was now finally able to say no, although in reality he was finally acting out his long-held lack of power and pushing his family away.

As I've pointed out, it is often the case that the real story behind troubling adult behavior is that the person is unconsciously acting out an issue resulting from his childhood conditioning. Through therapy, wherein the unconscious is brought to the surface, we can discover that the behavior made complete sense in the context of the person's early environment, but it doesn't make sense in today's adult world. This therapeutic enlightenment makes it clear that understanding your core conditioning helps you truly comprehend why you act the way you do today.

In Phil's case, his outward behavior was alienating those around him. But by understanding what motivated his inner child — the pressure of his birth order and the need to please his parents — one can see more clearly Phil's need to create boundaries around him where he could have some control in his life. Setting boundaries is important, but it is how you go about establishing them that makes the difference. Again, the key issue around the push-pull personality is the sense of not having control over the Self or the environment around you and the sense of abandonment when you do oppose those you love.

THE PASSIVE-AGGRESSIVE MATE

You've undoubtedly heard the term passive-aggressive, but what precisely does it mean? Here's a case that explains it quite well, especially in light of understanding how this behavior arises from the push-pull personality.

Jackie was a 41-year-old woman, married for 5 years without children. She came into therapy complaining that she often rages at her husband and can't help herself from doing so. He now wants to leave her. I asked her if she has always raged or was it just in this relationship. She replied that her anger indeed seemed more intense and severe in this relationship, but she admitted that she had been a "yeller" in other relationships.

When I asked her what she thought about her yelling, she confessed that she didn't feel good about her behavior, but she thinks that her husband doesn't hear her unless she yells. She starts off conversations with her husband in a perfectly normal way, she said, but when she feels that he doesn't hear her, she resorts to raising her voice. I asked for an example of an incident and she related the following. One day, she was sitting in the kitchen with her husband after a long day at work. She had just told him that she was tired from her day at work, when her husband asked what "they were doing for dinner."

At that point, she said, she became incensed with him. After all, she had just told him she was tired, so how could he dare ask what she was cooking for dinner. She felt he expected her to get up and cook, so she started to yell at him.

On the surface, Jackie may seem perfectly justified to yell at her husband for his insensitivity. However, I needed to explore more deeply to see if Jackie was truly reacting to her husband, or whether it might have been something else in her own past. After all, she really didn't need to yell at him for his question; a simple request for *him* to cook dinner might work or ordering out is another option. Furthermore, he had simply asked what "they were doing for dinner." He hadn't specifically told her to cook.

In talking about her background, I learned that Jackie was the only girl in a family of four. She loved her family and reported that she had a normal childhood, with parents who were actively involved with her schoolwork, her daily activities, and her social life. But she also reported that her mother worked during the day and so Jackie was expected to clean the house and cook many of the dinners. She claimed that she didn't mind helping out because her mom was tired when she got home, and the family had no maids or servants. Furthermore, since all her siblings were boys, they were not expected to help.

Up to this point in our conversation, Jackie showed no anger or feelings of resentment for having to care for her family. Yet in today's world, she frequently yells, which to me indicates a connection, even though she can't see it. To make the connection, I asked Jackie to recall if, as a child, she could ever refuse to clean the house or cook the meals, or if she could ask her brothers for help. She said no to all this, adding that she could never ask her brothers to help because they wouldn't even consider it. She now recalled that, in fact, she had to come home directly from school and could not play with her friends. When I asked her if she ever wanted to go out and play instead of having to return directly from school, she said of course, but that she had to do what was asked of her. I questioned if she ever was bothered by the demands placed on her, and she still stoically insisted that she just never allowed herself to think about it.

Jackie did not consciously realize that she continues to feel the demands of her childhood. When her husband simply asked what "they were doing for dinner," Jackie heard the words "What are you cooking?" And since, as a child, she could not say no to her mother and had to abide by her demand, she viewed her husband's statement as if it were her mother's. It didn't matter that her husband might have even been suggesting they go out to a restaurant. She heard his question as an assault on her freedom and thereby felt compelled to yell at him.

Jackie's case is a perfect example of passive aggressive behavior. The passive part is that she thought she had clearly communicated to her husband, when in fact she hadn't, because she was interpreting events as if she were still in her childhood. In her mind, telling her husband that "she was tired" meant that she had warned him that she didn't want to cook. The passive aspect is that, rather than saying "I don't want to cook tonight, she substituted "I am tired," and expected her husband to understand her message.

The aggressive part of Jackie's behavior is obviously the yelling, which has its roots in her childhood feelings of powerlessness and being forced into playing a household role she didn't want as a child. As a result, she now acts out aggressively, using yelling to tell her husband to stop. Her words and true message get lost because the rage is all her husband hears. Inside, Jackie feels tremendous pressure from her husband and assumes he is putting pressure on her, as her mother had done.

If you identify with this scenario, recognize again that passive-aggressive behavior is a confusing combination of indirectly saying what you feel rather than directly saying it, and then aggressively reacting as the result of feeling powerless over others. Both sides of your behavior trace back to your childhood and your inability to state directly what you feel as well as an attempt to relive and control the expectations placed on you back then. In all reality, you are not communicating clearly with your partner. As much as you may think your partner is to blame for the breakdowns in your relationship, it is far more likely that your own sense of powerlessness contributes to your problems.

THE WORKAHOLIC

Workaholism is actually a form of the push-pull personality, and may have its roots in a childhood upbringing that explicitly or implicitly creates tremendous pressure on a person to succeed. In some ways, a workaholic partner is almost the same as having a partner who has an addiction. Whether the addiction is work or drugs or alcohol, the underlying motive is escape.

Bob, a 38-year-old attorney, was married for one year and came to see me because he felt he had made a mistake and should never have married. He had known his wife for three years, during two of which they had lived together, before getting married.

Bob suddenly felt he shouldn't have gotten married. I asked Bob if he had plenty of time to assess whether something about his wife bothered him when they were dating and living together for the prior three years. He reported that they loved each other very much but that, once they were married, it just wasn't the same for him. I concluded that this was a case in which something was being triggered to cause Bob to detach so suddenly from the woman he reported to love and to have no previous real issues with.

As always, it was important to explore Bob's childhood. I learned that his parents were good to him, but extremely controlling and demanding. They told him what sports to play, what college to go to, even how to run his law practice. When I asked Bob if he could differ from his parents in what he wanted, he responded with a clear no. He knew about their control over him, and replied that he had tried in the past to get them to lay off him, but they always justified their actions by telling him, "we simply want the best for our son." Despite his anger though, Bob accepted the pressure and became very successful. He worked in an established legal practice, had a huge office, a fancy car, and all the trappings of wealth. On the surface, everything looked ideal.

Given his parents' high degree of involvement in his life and decision making, I wondered if Bob had problems with pressure on him elsewhere in his life. He told me that most of the time, he felt he owed his law firm for having given him a break and being good to him. As a result, he felt he could not say no to his firm, and so he took on many clients and worked long hours. This indicated to me that Bob was indeed sensitive to pressure from others, not just his wife.

By analogy, I asked Bob if he didn't feel that he "owed his wife" too? He thought a moment and said their situation was different because he felt he could never please her. She constantly complained about his working all the time. She complained whenever he had to travel for work. And she complained when he had early morning business meetings or stayed in the office late at night or worked weekends.

Clearly, when you are married, your spouse has expectations that you will be available, emotionally and physically, at least some of the time. So I asked Bob if he ever felt that any of his wife's needs were legitimate, or did he feel that she just never understood his need for work. He responded that when they were first dating and living together for those two years, he was around more often. But after they got married, his work increased and she just wasn't appreciative of his growing stature in the firm. He also maintained that his long hours of working benefited them in the money he earned, so why couldn't she appreciate his work rather than being depressed or sad that he was gone.

By this point, Bob's issues were getting clearer. On one hand, Bob seemed to be someone with simple marital problems, but in reality, he was dealing with unconscious historical parental pressure being repeated in today's world. Bob's new parent was his work, where he couldn't say no, just as he couldn't say no to his birth parents. Because he couldn't possibly say no at work, he had to hide his true personal needs, including his love for his wife.

As work consumed his life, he increasingly detached from his wife, not because he didn't love her, but because he didn't know how to stay attached to his wife without feeling pressure from the new parent – his work. He wanted his career to flourish, and he wanted his marriage to flourish but he came to see his wife's demands as forcing him to make a choice — her or work. Bob simply couldn't hear his wife's legitimate needs for connection, interpreting them as demands that must come secondary to the demands of his work. Work is what his parents valued, not his relationship.

In essence, Bob was not being true to himself. If he let go of work, he would feel cheated about his career. If he gave everything to his wife, he would lose his work.

What Bob – and many workaholics – need to understand is that a healthy life requires both your work and your relationship. Typically, however, the workaholic wants to be the good child who performs and then receives accolades. The person's drive is seeking to either repeat the stroking the child once received, or to try hard to achieve the compliments that the child never received. In either case, the behavior is driven by the child's need for recognition. It reflects not necessarily a desire to work, but a desire to be the obedient child. The fear of not performing outweighs any personal need for intimacy. We all know that nearly all workaholics at some point begin to resent their work and wish they had some aspects of their true Self back.

Unfortunately, workaholics tend to see the world in black and white, as either/or choices, just like in childhood. You may think you must choose between work or your spouse, but you don't. In truth, there are compromises available to you. There is an acceptable gray area, which contains both the outside expectations and the private world of your own needs and wants. Unless you learn to accept your own needs and wants in addition to wanting to please others, you may attach to someone, but you will never remain attached for fear of not meeting someone else's expectations.

THE DRINKER

You might already be guessing correctly that alcoholism is similar to workaholism, except for the fact that alcoholism has a genetic component in many people. But some drinkers may not be "genetic" alcoholics, and are actually acting out a push-pull tendency arising from their childhood conditioning.

Consider my client, Jim, a 28-year-old single male, who came into therapy claiming he didn't understand why he was so unhappy. He told me that he had a very good job with the airlines, and his main concern was that he could not find a steady girlfriend, largely because he had a drinking problem. He added that he did not have any difficulty finding girlfriends because of his good looks, but his dilemma was keeping one. Once women found out about his drinking problem, they dropped him.

I wanted to know more about the little boy inside Jim. After all, why would a young, bright, and attractive single male resort to drinking so much that he would alienate so many potential mates? What was his internal chaos about?

In working with other alcoholics, I've learned that they carry unconscious pain from their childhood conditioning that prevents them from experiencing their feelings. In terms of this book, it can often be traced back to having domineering or controlling parents who prevented the child from satisfying his or her needs during the separation-individuation phase. Again, it doesn't mean that the parents were malicious or intentionally aimed to hurt their child; the parents were simply more overbearing than the young child could tolerate. As a result, whatever the situation, children of such parents learn to "stuff their feelings," and it is this self-denial that gets carried over into their adulthood where they turn to alcohol to numb their feelings.

Jim confessed that he was a lot to handle as a child. While his older sister was calm and went along with the program, doing whatever she was told, Jim characterized himself as a terror. He was a precocious child who explored and got into everything.

Whatever she tried to do, his mother didn't know how to control him. She finally resorted to an apparatus that some parents use, a sort of harness that Jim frequently had to wear so his mother could control his whereabouts. And then his father died when he was about seven years old, leaving Jim, his sister, and mother alone.

Given that I always listen for the relationship between the parent and child, and to the parent's reaction to the child moving away, I heard something vital in Jim's explanation of his family. First of all, it was clear that Jim was an active, happy, inquisitive kid, but he was given a message on some level that his wants and questions were not okay. Although his mother probably never meant to give him this negative message, the extent to which she went to control him (forcing him to wear a harness) clearly suggested that Jim overwhelmed her.

As a child, Jim absorbed these messages without knowing it and assumed that his desires were wrong. After all, his mother had no problems with his sister, and after the father's death, the mother actually needed Jim to be even more compliant than before. As a result, Jim turned inward. Without realizing the role of his conditioning, he believed that he was not okay and that the only way he could be okay with himself was to numb his wants. At some point, and for reasons that may never be known, he began drinking, and eventually alcohol became his preferred method of suppressing the Self.

You do not need to be a drinker to identify with the above situation. If you turn to drugs, alcohol, work addictions, always keep yourself busy and emotionally unavailable, can't settle down and attach to one person, or you remain uncommitted, this same analysis applies to you. On some level, you were presented as a child with messages that suggested that you were not okay the way you were, and/or that your differences from your other family members were unacceptable to your parents. For you, receiving love was difficult because you felt that you were in constant conflict with the rest of your family. As a result, running away from your feelings in some form became your lifestyle.

CONCLUSION

Often times it is the "black sheep" of the family that is the healthy child. They may feel they are wrong and different, but their difference is that they want to be true to their Self. But as each of the above scenarios shows, the conflict often is that the individual wants and needs of the child are considered wrong to some degree.

It is this sense of wrongness, badness, lack of support, and punishment that causes a child to later carry into his or her adult life resentment with intimacy. The only previous attachment experience the person had was negative and controlling, so there is now a need to avoid repeating it again. The inner child doesn't realize that the adult has new choices and can balance his own wants with those of others without severe repercussions. If you are a push-puller, you can resolve this conflict by replacing the pushing away behavior that accompanies your child's sense of being out of control with an appreciation that life is no longer just black and white but rather filled with options and choices that might allow you to stay connected to your partner.

CHAPTER 4

THE DEPENDENT PERSONALITY

As you learned in Chapter 1, the dependent personality abandons his or her own needs in order to maintain receiving love from others. This type of personality dynamic arises from a childhood upbringing in which, during the separation /individuation phases when the infant wants to begin to separate from the primary caretaker, the mother or primary caretaker gives messages that it is not safe to physically or emotionally distance from her. She also gives messages that if you disobey her wishes, the repercussions will be harsh and severe resulting in the child's learning to either be obedient or risk the loss of approval from mother.

This need to make mother happy and ensure a connection with mother is central to the infant/child's decision making. Depending upon the strength of the child and depending upon the degree of repercussions expressed by the parent, the child is presented with two choices: 1) give up Self to ensure mother's love or 2) give up the connectedness with the parent to ensure the survival of the Self.

The dependent person chooses the first path, which results in loss of individual identity and separateness to varying degrees. The outcome is a person who remains merged, attached, bonded to the earlier caretaker, and now in adult life hears a spouse or partner repeating the message that to feel safe, he or she must remain attached.

It is important to remember that mothers don't generally set out to create dependent children. For some mothers, it may be that this is a learned behavior from their own background, or it may be that the mother feels justified because she herself sees the world as unsafe and wants to protect the child from harm. Whatever the underlying reason, the mother's fears or concerns result in keeping the child going against its own instinct. The child learns that it is easier to relinquish its own needs rather than fight. Dependent individuals can therefore be understood in terms of looking at the child's unconscious fears over the loss of mother's love if he or she decides to defy her.

This type of early conditioning usually continues to affect the dependent child's psyche throughout adolescence and into adulthood. This happens because little has usually changed in the conditioning response from the parent(s) during these years. Fearing further repercussions, such people continue to act upon an unconscious pattern of behavior in which it is easier to see their own desires as secondary to others. They frequently give up their needs in favor of pleasing others in their life. They are driven by an unconscious fear of losing love and support from others if they do not yield to their needs.

Keep in mind that the fear of loss of love doesn't mean that the child or adult isn't emotionally capable of being on it's own. Rather the child turned adult has learned not to get in touch with his or her strengths and therefore doesn't really know what they are capable of.

It is often the case that when I get a so-called dependent individual, they are extremely bright and psychologically capable of greater things. They simply haven't tapped their strengths and therefore feel inadequate. The only real issue that keeps them from pushing out of their dependent frame of reference is the underlying fear of being wrong, bad, selfish, or alone because they want something different than what other's have historically wanted for them.

Dependent people may eventually face serious problems and unhappiness in their adult relationships because their pattern of stifling their own needs is all they know. In their relationships with their spouse and children, the dependent person's family may or may not want to participate in their dependency paradigm. Problems arise within the family when family members react negatively to the degree to which they may be asked to acquiesce.

Here are some examples of how dependent personalities experience different types of adult relationship conflicts. As you read these cases, remember that the primary fear that motivates these people is the loss of love when they exercise their own wants and therefore giving in is simply easier than fighting.

THE "IF YOU LOVE ME, YOU'LL GIVE UP EVERYTHING" PARTNER

This type of dependent personality actually represents a paradoxical behavioral pattern. This is the classic type of personality you so often see of someone who bosses others around but whose actions actually reflect a deep-seated insecurity at their core. On the surface, this person seems domineering and manipulative, constantly asserting his or her needs, while expecting everyone around to abandon their desires. However, what lies beneath this person's outer veneer is an insecure, dependent child who attempts to control others because he or she experienced this same type of love growing up. They are simply repeating what they know. Their background was wrought with domination and surrender and therefore they do to others what was done to them.

Consider Betty, a 45-year old woman who came to see me because she couldn't understand why her marriage was in such terrible trouble. She had been married for nearly twenty years and claimed she loved her family very much and only wanted the best for them. However, she also admitted that her husband and children were angry with her most of the time. As we talked about her situation, Betty then shared with me that her husband often referred to her as the "warden."

Here was clearly a clue into the dynamics of Betty's problem: in her family's eyes, she was viewed as domineering and pushy. As you've seen throughout this book, a deeper issue usually exists that explains the real truth operating in someone's psyche. The fact that Betty's family referred to her as the warden actually revealed less about her domineering personality than it revealed about her hidden unresolved issues.

As a therapist, I began to think that what was really going on behind Betty's domineering exterior was an attempt to force her family to need her. In essence, Betty was requiring her family to follow and imitate her, reflecting her deep-seated needs to receive their love through their devotion to her in the same way her earlier conditioning reflected a devotion to her family.

As mentioned in Chapter 1, personality types are often passed on from one generation to another. A push-pull mother often raises a push-pull child; a dependent mother is likely to raise a dependent child. The behavioral pattern is often repeated from one generation to the next, and may conceivably go on for decades if unchecked. I therefore wanted to see how Betty's upbringing was played out to create her dependent and controlling dynamic.

As we talked, Betty revealed that when she grew up, her grandmother lived near them. As a result, Betty's mother was always expected to help her mother. Betty's mother was so devoted to her own mother that she lived her life for her. Unfortunately, this got passed down to Betty, and she was expected to do the same for her mother who she had lived near for much of her own family life.

Although Betty's mother had now died, Betty was clearly continuing to live out the same pattern with her own husband and children, asking them to take care of her in the same way that her mother was asked to take care of her grandmother. This lifestyle was so ingrained in Betty that she did not see anything wrong with expecting her family to give up all their own wants and needs for her. Given her upbringing, she saw this family rule as normal and common. In her eyes, all children should willingly give up their wants and needs for their mother.

As mentioned above, the psychological irony being played out here was that Betty's attempt to dominate her family in asking that they abandon their wants in favor of hers was the exact opposite of what she had wanted for her loved ones. She consciously never wanted her family to feel the pressure of performing in the same way she felt the pressure of showing up for her mother. Yet Betty was actually creating a dynamic in which she was unconsciously living out the dependency taught by her mother. Of course, she did not realize that her domineering behavior alienated the entire family rather than attracted their love.

It is possible that, despite being domineering, Betty could have been living in a happy marriage. However, she was in conflict with her husband and children because they were not eager to abandon the ways in which they wanted to lead their lives. Betty's husband was apparently not used to the degree of self-sacrifice that Betty required from those around her. As the years went by, all he could see was a wife constantly harping on him, rather than a woman who desperately sought his love in the only form she knew how.

In addition, her husband's negative reactions to Betty were being consciously or unconsciously transmitted to their children over the years. The husband's resistance to Betty's dependency effectively prevented the behavior from being transmitted to the children. They grew up exposed to a different, healthier message from their father and did not "inherit" the types of early conditioning that Betty had received from her mother and grandmother. This made the children even more resistant to showing Betty the love she wanted in the way she wanted it. Everyone suffered due to the unconscious manner in which Betty's childhood conditioning was affecting the way in which people interacted with one another.

Given these dynamics, Betty was stuck in a marriage in which it appeared to her that no one appreciated how she sacrificed for them. In her mind, no one listened to her requests, which were actually requests for love. She felt isolated from her husband and children and had no clue as to why. She also believed that her loving family was breaking apart and so she lashed out further trying to save it.

Thus began a vicious circle of family dysfunction. Each time Betty asked for something from her family, she expected to get it without anyone questioning her. But each time her husband or children said no, she responded by becoming silent and withdrawing, or by getting angry. In her mind, the family was selfish. She expected them to obey her wishes just as she had obeyed her mothers.

As you can see, Betty's situation was complex and paradoxical. She needed to cut through multiple layers of her past to see that behind her domineering motherly role was a dependent little girl who was taught to want unconditional love from her family. Betty had to first understand that all her needs were not always legitimate and that she could not continue expecting her family to fulfill them. She also had to learn that she was trying to punish her family by withdrawing or getting angry, just as a child attempts to do, whenever she felt they were disappointing her.

I worked with Betty to discover and heal her past with her mother and grandmother. I focused on helping Betty recognize that, as a child, she did not always agree with her own mother, nor want to do exactly what her mother expected of her. Such therapeutic discussion allowed some of Betty's childhood anger and resentment to come out, as she realized that her mother was the byproduct of her own conditioning with Betty's grandmother. Little by little, Betty could see that she was playing out the same scenario that her mother played out with grandmother, and that she had played out with her own mother. She realized that her expectations of others did not consider their wants and desires and that she would therefore emotionally abandon them whenever their actions disappointed her.

Betty's therapy proved successful, as she discovered over time that her family truly wanted to love her but they simply didn't want to sacrifice themselves to get it. The more flexible Betty was, the more loving and attentive her family became. She eventually found that she got much more out of them by not being demanding and not threatening to withdraw her love. One of the best outcomes of Betty's therapy was that her family stopped referring to her as the warden.

THE WITHDRAWING LOVE PARTNER

In Chapter 3, you saw how withdrawing from your partner can be a sign of a push-pull personality who suddenly becomes afraid to remain in the relationship. However, withdrawal can also be a sign of a dependent personality whose dependency is so great that even the slightest problem in a relationship causes the person to create distance and avoid regular communication.

The feeling here is that the adult is afraid to oppose their partner's wants. The opposition represents going against the "parent" and earlier experiences from childhood clearly conditioned the child now adult to fear reprisal. On the outside, the person is saying nothing except to withdraw, but on the inside, the person is really saying "I don't agree with you but I am afraid to tell you and have you not love me".

Tony, a 40 year-old man married for seven years, wanted to leave his marriage. However, he was afraid that in divorcing his wife he would abandon his 10-year old daughter. The problem was, Tony was very unhappy and felt his wife controlled him all the time. Although he sometimes thought that he loved his wife and they shared many activities and a common lifestyle, he felt he could no longer tolerate her domination over him.

When I first hear someone report that they fear their partner, two things go through my mind. Is the partner truly someone to fear, arising perhaps out of physical or mental abuse, or is the person who fears their partner afraid to come to the plate? Most often, the dependent person's conditioning created a fear to express himself or herself. They want to avoid what they assume will happen, which is conflict. Any disagreement is viewed as a negative and therefore to be avoided at all costs.

When a couple has been married for several years, it can be extremely insightful to detect if a specific event triggered a change in their perceptions of their partner or if a pattern existed from the outset of the relationship. I therefore asked Tony if he could recall their dating patterns and the early years of their marriage.

Tony thought a moment and said that things were generally fine when they were first dating and into the first two years of their marriage, but then his wife began to act differently, though he didn't know why. I asked what about her behavior had changed. He felt she began to be disapproving of him and that he felt he could not longer please her. I prodded Tony to think deeply about what events had happened at that time. Suddenly, he realized that this was the year when their daughter was born. This made sense to me, because childbirth – especially a first child -- is often a watershed experience in creating conflict for couples.

As Tony reflected on the early years of his daughter's childhood, he recalled that he and his wife began constantly disagreeing about how to parent their child. Tony said his wife was always telling their child what to do, what to wear, and how to be. In his mind, his wife was constantly "at her," never letting the child venture out on her own or experiment freely with life. Tony laughed as he reported that this was also the time when his wife began treating him much the same way.

At first glance, you might be tempted to think that Tony's wife needed control and thus clearly the cause of their problems. And in fact that issue needs to be explored. However, remember again that it is important to look at how both parties have issues that play a role in a relationship dynamic. In this situation, I wondered whether she was really too controlling and/or if Tony was hyper-sensitive to his wife's attitude which he viewed as controlling, which indicated that something in his background was reoccurring for him.

In other words, Tony's sensitivity to control was a tip off that he might also have his own issue about control, not just his wife. I felt that his powerlessness to approach his wife told me a lot about him. When a person avoids communicating out of fear that they will anger their partner, it is a red flag about their past conditioning. It immediately tells me that whether or not their partner is wrong is not as critical as getting the dependent person to move more into their adult and verbalize without the fear of consequences.

In this case, Tony's child remains in control even today, and so my therapy focused on getting Tony to understand that his approach arises from his child, not his adult. An adult can walk away, disagree without fear of saying something wrong, etc. Tony was living life from a more primitive helpless position fearing his own feelings might upset his wife and she would then go away. In reality the only one that was going away was Tony.

I asked Tony if anything in his past might have made him sensitive to how he perceived his wife controlling their daughter. He responded without delay that it reminded him of his own mother who controlled everything around him when he was growing up. He recalled being forbidden to do a lot of activities that he wanted to participate in because his mother was afraid he would get hurt. In the end, Tony said that as a child, he just gave in to his mother's wishes to make her happy. He admitted that he did a little bit of rebelling during his high school years but it was short lived. He soon returned to being the obedient son, which was how he thought of himself even today.

It was clear to me that Tony was actually reliving his own past through his daughter. Whenever his wife would tell their daughter what to do, Tony felt that he himself was being controlled. Just as his mother controlled him, he believed that his wife's control was cheating his daughter from doing what she wanted to do. Given Tony's early conditioning of feeling deprived, controlled, and withheld from, it was natural that he wouldn't want his only child to experience the same.

The problem was, Tony's reaction to his perception of his wife controlling their daughter was to withdraw. He would come home late from work or find reasons to be away from his wife whenever he was angry with her. His actions were clearly not a prescription for a healthy marriage. Withdrawing from communicating your feelings to your partner doesn't address or solve the root causes of your problems. Whether or not Tony's wife was truly overbearing was less important than the fact that Tony could not find it in himself to communicate clearly with her about his feelings to see how receptive his wife might be.

At first, Tony had difficulty seeing that he was reliving issues from his own early conditioning. He had to find out if his wife would withdraw if he spoke up. What he found was that his wife was actually more pliable than he imagined. In fact, up until now, Tony had never tested the waters of telling his wife how he felt about her control of their daughter. He automatically assumed she was closed to his objections, which made him withdraw his love whenever he perceived her to be controlling. He simply had never given her a chance because he would shut down whenever he became upset just as he did in his early years.

Through therapy, Tony learned that his wife was actually quite approachable and open to his input. While they didn't always agree, their lines of communication exceeded anything Tony had ever expected. And after therapy, Tony no longer wanted to leave his wife. He admitted that from time to time, he could feel himself regressing back to feeling like a helpless child, unable to speak his mind or contradict his wife's wants. But most of the time, Tony was able to keep himself in check by realizing whenever he got upset that he was reliving his own issues while his wife was actually a loving, constant, caring mother who at times simply needed to learn how to give up her control tendencies.

THE INVISIBLE PARTNER

Perhaps you know people who seem invisible. They do not have a career drive, interests, or hobbies. They seem meek and unassuming. They have no wants or needs. Sharing life with such people is difficult, because you never know what they think or feel. More importantly, the burden is on you to make them happy.

Such people are, in essence, a sub-type of the dependent personality in which their early conditioning strongly taught them not to express their personality. The fear of being themselves and owning their feelings is a sign that the child within them of long ago was not allowed to fully exist. Difficulty with self-expression and silence suggests that parental criticism, negative input, or punishment had a strong enough impact on the person's inner child as to prevent them from fully being themselves.

The timid inner child-like behavior then becomes the modus operandi for that person, even in adulthood. Paradoxically, people often continue to create their own inner turmoil, because this is all they have known and therefore they continue their behavior because this is what feels safe to them. In a kind of negative feedback loop, they continue to create the same childhood emotional absences to life because these responses support their long-term position of this behavior as the only way to feel safe.

Consider the case of Susan, a 38-year old married woman who came to me because "life just wasn't working." Her speech was slow and cautious, and it was in fact difficult to understand what exactly was troubling her. As she spoke she told me that she was in a relationship that allowed her to operate comfortably as a passive person. She related that her husband felt that he had to guess what her wants might be and fulfill them. He complained that she never wanted for anything and that he didn't know what would make her happy. He told Susan that she wasn't fully enjoying her relationship herself, or experiencing all that life had to offer.

We began exploring Susan's childhood, and she reported that her mother helped her in making decisions for her. Susan told me that her mother decided what college she would attend, what major she would choose, and what sport she would play in. She didn't report this in a way that seemed troubling to Susan. Typically when a mother continues to make these important personal decisions for a woman in her 20's, one can correctly assume that the mother was highly controlling throughout that woman's childhood and adolescence. Yet, Susan didn't seem to mind. In fact she was grateful that mother helped her because she felt she couldn't have made these decisions on her own.

Susan reported that she had hardly dated and never really opened up to anyone, until she met her husband who was the first man to be very patient with her, not pushing her beyond what she wanted to do. In fact, she admitted that he was so supportive that even she wondered how he put up with her silence and withdrawal for so long. She knew he was unhappy despite the fact that he never complained to her. She finally said that one reason for coming into therapy was that she felt guilty about cheating him out of his life. She knew she was acting inappropriately as a wife and it hurt her to see the man she loved suffering so much.

Susan truly wanted to get out of her skin at this point in her life, but she just didn't know how. And she didn't know why she was like this. I began exploring the separation process to see if and how her early conditioning might have made her feel afraid of being herself. Again I want to emphasize that when I explore the past it is not to place blame. It is simply my attempt at understanding the adult's reactions to conditioning and to know where and why they are stuck. Upon understanding why we do what we do a person then has an understanding of their journey to mental health.

Susan started talking about her upbringing and described her mother and father as loving parents who were constantly busy running the family business. She said they were good parents and provided her with everything she would want but that they had very little time for her. She saw them as overwhelmed and she didn't want to add to their burden by making any waves or causing any more hardship on them. She reported to me that she wanted to make her parents proud of her and didn't want to cause conflict. They already had a lot of conflict in meeting the bills each month and working long hours.

To help around the house, Susan was asked to come home directly from school and clean the house and cook for mother. I asked Susan if she ever wanted to go out and play instead of just coming home. She said yes but wouldn't dare ask. I asked why not. She reported that mother would get angry and yell a lot. She felt again that mother was too overwhelmed and didn't want to upset her further.

Susan therefore grew up spending long hours alone and working within the house to contribute to making life easier for her parents. She simply had no wants or needs of her own and did what was expected of her. When decisions needed to be made she let mother make them. She was sure that mother knew what was right for her and that making mother happy was her goal. And avoiding mother's temper was also her goal.

Within a few therapy sessions, Susan became very aware that she was driven by a need to please and avoid conflict, which related to mother getting mad. Her solution was so severe that in effect she abandoned her own wants by virtually having no wants or needs of her own. She began to understand that her invisible behavior was a reaction to her upbringing within the family, an outgrowth of not wanting to cause waves, wanting to please, and wanting to avoid conflict. She learned to give back to her parents by not having any of her own needs or wants other than what she was told she could have. She learned to live life according to what her parent's needs were and not have any of her own.

Fortunately, she could see now that in today's world she needed to learn how to be more present. She loved her husband and didn't want to continue hurting him any more. By understanding how her need to please her parents and avoid mother's feelings of being upset had created in her an absent adult, Susan realized that she had to begin to test the waters of opening up and coming to the plate with her husband. Little by little, they began to talk more, share more, and love each other more easily. Needless to say, her husband was very receptive, as he truly loved her. Today Susan remains happily married and continues to work on not going back to her old patterns of non-existence that hurt her marriage and her entire life.

THE SUBMISSIVE PARTNER

The submissive partner is perhaps the most obvious type of dependent personality. This type of person continuously submits to his spouse or partner's needs, without trying to have his own needs met as well, or without seeking a compromise between the two of them.

Take Brad, for example, a 60- year old man who had been with the same woman for forty years. He came to my office one day and explained that it was not in his character to step into a therapist's office, but there was something he could no longer take. We began chatting and he revealed that he had married his high school sweetheart. Together, he and his wife Connie had lived full lives, raising four children. He was now retiring from his career as an accountant, and was looking forward to his golden years. But he had come to the conclusion that he wanted a divorce and didn't know what to do.

I could see Brad was exploding inside, and I wanted to understand why so I asked him to elaborate on what was going on with his marriage. He had stayed married for forty years and I wanted to know why now he wanted a divorce. Brad explained that for all the years they were married and raising a family, he would literally escape from his wife through his work so he wouldn't have to deal with her. But now that he was retired and was often in the house with her, he could no longer stand being with her.

I asked Brad what exactly did his wife do that alienated him so much. Brad reflected and said tearfully that Connie took great care of their kids, provided them with security and love, and she always showed up at all their activities while they grew up. But the whole family paid a heavy price, he said sadly, in that Connie was overbearing and frequently "raged" at them when she became upset. "I was able to handle it only because I simply left and went to work," Brad admitted sheepishly. "That was my way of shutting her out. And I feel bad, because I left the kids to fend for themselves."

Brad's inability to deal with his wife's raging was as much a concern to me as hearing about his wife's inappropriate reactions. Even without knowing why his wife raged, how often, or in what manner, the most important element here was our need to understand if Brad had ever addressed his marital problems before? Whenever I hear from clients that they have allowed inappropriate behaviors to persist for a long time, I automatically question what in their earlier conditioning has prevented them from speaking up. I look for clues that might relate their adult behavior back to their separation experience or to transferences from their past that suggest a familiar experience that now repeats itself over and over.

We began discussing Brad's childhood and family experience. He revealed that he came from a family where mother ruled the roost. His father was passive and emotionally unavailable, and so Brad learned to go along with his mother's wishes just to make her happy. He also saw that his other role model, his father, simply retreated into his newspaper rather than assert himself with his wife. I asked Brad what would have happened if he had spoken up and voiced his opinions to his mother. He replied that she would have become very upset and her anger was enough to keep him quiet. In short, it was clear that Brad had grown up feeling that letting his mother have her way was both easier and his only alternative. He learned to be submissive, just like his father, preferring to clam up rather than fear the abandonment of his mother's love. Thus, a dependency model took root in his psyche.

Whether or not Brad's wife Connie was a rager, Brad himself needed to make some serious changes in himself. I suggested that before he made any radical decisions about leaving his wife after all these years, he needed to work on his own issues first. He had to move out of this submissive mode of being and stop fearing the repercussions from his "love object," whether it was his mother or his wife. Brad's first step was therefore to share his feelings with his wife whenever he disagreed with her or wanted to say something whether he thought she would like it or not. He had to stop being afraid that she would stop loving him, no matter what he said or did to her.

It can be very difficult to make changes after living a long life as a submissive person, but it is not impossible. People can and do change. Internally, the human mind has an innate desire to want to be happier. And we have a responsibility to ourselves to evolve. We are all presented with tests in life and the degree to which we conquer them will determine the degree of happiness we get out of life itself. The degree of happiness we seek differs greatly between people, with some of us demanding a lot for ourselves, while others worry more about the other person than themselves, while still others simply check out from life. In this case, Brad may never be a man who shares all his feelings, but he had the ability to change the degree to which he withdrew.

I asked Brad to begin by establishing a clear boundary between him and his wife, letting her know that he would no longer tolerate her raging. He had to learn to speak up to her using his adult mind, not his inner child's brain in which he saw himself as a victim of his upbringing

In this situation, it also helped that Brad's children wanted their Dad to change. They were thrilled that he was seeking therapy and supported him a great deal.

As Brad finally opened up to his wife, the two began to have truly honest dialogues that helped them understand each other far beyond their forty years together. Connie admitted to Brad that she hadn't realized how bad she really was, but that she felt frustrated all those years because he was always retreating to his office, leaving her with all the responsibilities of raising the family. Her statement in fact led Brad to see that he actually contributed to his own problems, so it was not truly all "her fault." Through their honest sharing of feelings, the two spouses began to truly communicate and break through their blocks. They also came closer together as a couple and soon stopped fearing the other's loss of love.

THE PASSIVE-AGGRESSIVE PARTNER

In Chapter 3, you learned that passive aggressive indicates that the person has a two-sided behavioral pattern in communicating his or her wants to others. First, the person does not directly communicate his or her feelings, but instead unconsciously expects other people to sense or understand what he or she is feeling through their indirect communication. Next, when others do not do what the person expected, he or she becomes overly angry and upset with them.

Brad's wife, Connie, who you just read about, is an example of a passive aggressive dependent personality. As you saw in reading Brad's case, Connie raged at her family because she felt she was burdened with the responsibilities of raising the family without help from her absent husband. Her rage was her aggressive behavior. However, at other times, Connie would retreat into her bedroom where she would become silent and withdrawn for hours. This was her passive behavior, with which she was expecting to communicate to her family that she was unable to handle her hurt feelings. Of course, no one understood that her withdrawals were her attempt to communicate her feelings.

Connie agreed to work with me in therapy just as I did with Brad. My first question for her was the same as for Brad: why in forty years hadn't she simply told her husband that she needed more help from him? What was going on inside her emotionally that kept her vacillating between withdrawal and rage, never thinking that a healthier alternative was easily available to her if she could just communicate straightforwardly to Brad.

I knew that something in Connie's background must have been triggered that she would never reveal her true emotions to her family. In delving into her early years, Connie reported that she was the oldest of five children. Her father worked and so her mother was saddled with raising this large clan of kids. As a result, Connie's mother delegated many of the family responsibilities to

Connie. She was charged with taking care of the home and tending to some of the children. When Connie was young, she had to do the cooking and cleaning. As she got older and was able to drive, she was asked to drive her siblings to and from school. In the end, Connie spent much of her childhood and high school years putting her own needs aside to care for her family and meet the requests of mother.

When I pressed Connie to explain why she never spoke up to her mother, she finally shared with me that her mother was an alcoholic who drank at night. Connie feared that if she spoke up, her mother would drink even more and that scared her. She explained that her mother was very responsible during the day, but once her father came home, her mother felt her day was done and she turned to alcohol. She would then get angry when she was drinking, or she would simply drink until she passed out. In either case, her mother controlled Connie unknowingly through, on the one hand, demanding that Connie help out, and on the other hand, making Connie fear that she would drink even more.

As you might guess, Connie's adult family life today was closely imitating her childhood years. She continued to be the homemaker for a large family, which reinforced in her mind a sense that she was once again saddled with too many responsibilities. Meanwhile, she perceived her husband as being able to escape from the family to his work. The problem was, Connie couldn't discuss her feelings with Brad, just as she couldn't speak up as a child to tell her mother that she didn't want to do everything or that it was too much to ask of her. In some ways, she also believed that her mother was overburdened herself and that not helping her was out of the question, so that now as adult, she was not entitled to get help either.

Connie was bringing her past into her present. Furthermore, she was so used to her role as caregiver that she simply didn't feel anything else was possible. As a result, raging became her only outlet for venting her feelings. Getting angry was in effect her way of finally saying no to her mother and to Brad. Because she didn't know how to discuss her feelings with them, her rage was her way of communicating. Furthermore, although her fear of mother's alcoholic abyss was no longer there, since her husband was not an alcoholic, Connie probably sensed that Brad was a workaholic, so she equally feared losing him even more frequently to his work if she spoke up.

As Connie understood more about her patterns of behavior and why she raged at her family, she began to see that all she needed to do was to speak up more. With better communication for both of them, she and Brad learned to be truthful about their feelings and ultimately saved their marriage.

CONCLUSION

In the cases in this chapter, you saw how the fear of loss of love or abandonment is the underlying feature of the dependent personality. That fear stops people from being true to themselves in life, able to communicate their wants and desires without worrying that others will stop loving them for doing so. For such people, the dependent inner child remains in charge of their adult life, and they continue to feel helpless and powerless in many situations. Helplessness is a sense of being out of control over the feared or eventual loss of love. Powerlessness is the result of not being able to change their parents' behavior or stop the abuse being infringed on them.

The treatment for the dependent individual is to realize that they can survive outside of their parent's sphere without constantly having a dreaded primitive fear of being annihilated. By getting stronger and whole within themselves, the dependent person can become ever more present and true to themselves.

CHAPTER 5

THE WAVERING PERSONALITY

So far, I have presented cases that depict people stuck in either the push-pull personality or the dependent personality. But given that personalities are not stagnant and don't always fit tightly into pigeonholes, it happens that some people fall into a gray area – the wavering personality. As you recall, this dynamic refers to someone who vacillates between the extremes of, on one hand, excessive attachment, neediness, or relinquishing of the Self to secure love, and on the other hand, not attaching at all but rather fleeing away.

In this chapter, we will explore cases in which people go between these two extremes. When you live with this type of wavering personality, you can be frequently off balance and never feel quite settled into the relationship because your mate seems very unpredictable, no matter how well you may know him or her. In a sense, you never know what you are going to get when you partner with a wavering personality. Sometimes the wavering person can be very loving and emotionally close; but then, without any warning, the person's mood changes and he or she suddenly detaches from you.

Where does this wavering come from, and why? Let me review the background of the wavering personality. In childhood, more often then not, the wavering person experienced many instances of feeling overpowered and controlled, as well as many instances of feeling loved and supported. When the messages were negative, the child didn't know how to stop the intrusion of the parent (whether they consciously recognize it or not) so it learned to retreat into itself for safety. Now, as an adult, the wavering person's attachment moves between feeling close and loving to feeling smothered, burdened, and overpowered. This leads the person to seek detachment as the only safe haven. Essentially, the adult continues to unconsciously repeat this pattern of flight whenever they believe people are asking too much of them. In reality, the partner's requests for closeness and intimacy may not be excessive, but to the eyes of the wavering person, other people's requests for attachment feel like a net is being pulled in around them. "Flee, Flee Flee" is their fighting song.

Here are some cases that illustrate how a wavering personality can act out this pattern while in a relationship.

The "Sign on the Dotted Line" Personality

Are you in a relationship that began in a wonderful, romantic dating period, but as soon as you married the person, everything changed? Well, this type of situation is not as unusual as you might think. In fact, it is so common that I refer to it as the "sign on the dotted line person."

Meet Joe. He dated his girlfriend for roughly two years, then they married. The two of them were married for seven months when Joe came to see me. He wanted to leave his wife.

Up to the time of marriage, Joe told me, both partners believed the relationship to be truly wonderful. They seldom had any conflicts, and they enjoyed each other's company immensely. But marriage seemed to have changed their bliss, according to Joe.

So what happened? Prior to marrying, Joe said that he and Julie lived separately. But once they began living together, he began to notice several things that greatly upset him. In fact, he found it impossible to live with his new wife. Although she kept a clean house, her closet was an absolute mess, with her clothes and supplies spilling into their bedroom. Joe asked Julie time and time again to clean up her stuff but his pleas were to no avail. Joe also complained to me that Julie would go into their kitchen late at night, have a snack, and then forget to clean her dishes. When he awoke, the sink was full of her plates and cutlery.

As Joe talked, it became clear that order was very important to him. For some reason, he needed to run a tight ship, so he experienced his wife's messiness as chaos overlapping into his world. The issue around order was not as much a concern for me, as the degree to which order blurred his desire to stay attached. I was therefore interested in knowing what in his background motivated these feelings in him? Even if it were true that Julie was less than a neat person, I still needed to understand why her stuff spilling over into his world made such a difference to Joe that it could turn off his feelings for his new wife. Was the messy closet the real issue, or was something in Joe ticking?

Let me interject here and tell you something about what I think when I have these types of situations. When a client reports that they want to leave their marriage, I begin by saying that, of course, it is their decision. But I remind them that separation and divorce can always happen, yet it is a more important to not react impulsively and to spend some time now to figure out if a decision to separate is being made for the right reasons. I invite my clients to look at themselves so they can learn to what degree their own unresolved issues play a role in the marital breakdown. Only after looking at their own "stuff" and understanding what really may be triggering their partner can a person decide what they can and cannot live with, before calling it quits.

I also remind clients that their own stuff will always follow them into their next relationship. When a person ups and leaves their current partner and finds a new one, their own issues will always accompany them right into the next relationship. In Joe's case, the messy closets and sink may go away, but Joe's issue around intrusions into his world will surface again. Since he has already an attachment to someone he once believed he loved, why go through the turmoil of divorcing, but then repeat the same patterns with someone else? The idea of already having an investment in a relationship usually makes sense to most people and causes them to want to work in therapy to identify their own issues.

In this case, I asked Joe to work with me to discover what triggers might be at work in his psyche. We knew that he felt safe while dating his wife, and only after she moved in did things change for him. This was our starting point. So we began exploring the issue concerning why Joe was so upset with his wife's messiness. Joe admitted feeling powerless whenever his wife disregarded his requests to keep an orderly house. He simply could not learn to live with this situation, he told me.

As I delved into Joe's past, the reasons became clear very quickly. Joe recalled how his family moved constantly when he was growing up. By the time he had graduated high school, Joe had gone to 10 schools. His family was constantly living in chaos, with boxes and papers scattered everywhere in his homes because his parents believed that the family was going to move soon again. They never made a real commitment to having their home look neat and tidy.

Throughout much of his childhood, Joe therefore felt helpless, especially around two issues. First, he detested moving so much and he was never part of the decision making. Every time he got settled in school he would have to uproot. Even as a kid, he seldom could do his own thing. Everything in his family's life was dictated by their moving around the country, as his dad seemed to always go from job to job.

Secondly, Joe always wished his family would take better care of their environment. He told me that he frequently asked his parents to pay attention to how their house looked, but no one seemed to care. In fact, Joe was often the brunt of jokes from his family, since he was the only one who had a "neatness" problem. Even in his own room, Joe felt that he had no control to keep things orderly, as he liked, because there was never enough room for everything.

Given the above, what Joe was experiencing today as an adult was as clear as day. He felt the same sense of powerlessness and intrusiveness as in his childhood because the love of his life encroached upon his space and disregarded his desire for orderliness. Each time his wife failed to hear Joe's pleas, his sense of powerlessness to change the chaos of his childhood returned. The only way for Joe to find relief was to close off emotionally, essentially fleeing from her just as he did in childhood.

What made Joe a wavering personality though was that he had a Dr. Jeckyl and Mr. Hyde duality about his marriage. Whenever he was not triggered, he was actually a very loving and emotionally connected husband. In fact, he told me that he was sometimes so needy for his wife's attention that she complained of not having time to do her own things. But whenever he saw her chaos, his powerlessness became triggered. It was like a switch going off in his brain, and he immediately changed into a different person. His tone became angry, he no longer felt loving, and he all but detached himself from her completely.

I worked with Joe to help him understand how his adult self was reliving the helplessness of his childhood years. Like so many wavering personalities, Joe needed to recognize that other people, including his spouse, could not be aware of doing things that triggered him so violently. Joe needed to open a dialogue with his wife to help her understand his trigger points and to define his boundaries.

With therapy, Joe learned to share more with his wife. They discussed his upbringing and his response to that upbringing, and they looked at her actions that today trigger him in the same way. Joe still needed order in his life, but the difference now was that both he and his wife could understand what was beneath Joe's Dr. Jeckyl/Mr. Hyde-like behavior. Joe worked especially on communicating his needs and boundaries rather than fleeing whenever he felt triggered.

Like so many wavering people, finding a flaw in the other person is often a symptom of their underlying need to escape. Putting the person down is clearly a way to create distance when the wavering person doesn't want to be completely attached but simply needs to find some safety in a brief flight away. In fact, this is the most common and subtle form of detachment-causing distance to break the feeling of being smothered or trapped. For Joe, given the degree of lack of control and change in his early years, he will always have to monitor his sense of powerlessness in situations. Whenever he gets triggered, he wants to control his environment. Instead of finding fault over the clothes or messiness, he needs to identify when he feels too invaded or unsafe.

I want to point out again that when I work with couples, I often find it much more beneficial to meet with both parties to understand the dynamics being acted out. In doing so, each spouse reveals their own material to me as they share how they see the other. As I begin to uncover what material is being acted out and why, I try to explain to both parties what unresolved issues they are facing. In this case, Joe's wife's ability to empathize with Joe greatly improved their situation. Much to his surprise, his wife fully agreed to be more careful picking up her clothes and being more in touch with the things she could do to make Joe feel a sense of order in his life. On the other hand, Joe agreed to identify for her when his moods changed so she would know it was a sign that he was feeling overwhelmed.

THE "MY BAGS ARE PACKED" PERSONALITY

Did you ever hear of a child who runs away from home, but then soon comes back? This is a form of the wavering personality that can sometimes become an adult dynamic, though the adult's version of running away is often more emotional than physical.

Take Bruce. One day when he was five years old, he made himself a peanut butter and jelly sandwich, packed his little suitcase, and left... at least for a short while. Upon his return, he rang the doorbell and when his mother came to the door, he told her sternly, "I'm going to give you one more chance."

Bruce's life hasn't changed much through the years. Today, he was married, no children, sometimes happy, but every once in a while he ran away, emotionally. This seemed to be his only way to cope with the minor problems in his marriage. Sometimes he would even get quite carried away, threatening to leave. Finally his wife, Rachel, demanded that they attend therapy to figure out what was going on with their three-year old marriage.

When Bruce started the therapy, he began by telling me that his wife didn't feel safe with him. He thought she feared that he would leave her. But he also told me that he didn't plan to leave her, he simply needed to run away some of the time. Bruce wondered if perhaps he was just afraid of commitment.

Again, when I hear that someone wants to flee a relationship, I automatically think of the person feeling trapped for some reason and needing to run for safety. After all, why does someone need to run away from a relationship just because they are upset or don't like something? It is only when one feels overpowered and small that one feels the need to escape.

I asked Bruce to tell what was troubling him about his wife. He said she was busy all the time and would often find fault with him. He felt she was always getting angry at him whenever he did something that she didn't like. When I asked him if he had told her about his dissatisfaction with her behavior, Bruce said no. I asked him why not, and he simply said he didn't want to rock the boat and get her angrier than she already was. Now I needed to know what was real. Was she a domineering and controlling woman raging at times? And even if the answer was yes, did Bruce's withdrawal contribute to his problems?

As I've stressed throughout this book, what matters most is your ability to communicate your feelings and how your feelings are received by your mate. The more you can appropriately communicate your feelings, the more adult and safe you are within yourself. And the more your partner openly receives the communication, the healthier the relationship.

Wavering people may or may not risk communication, but often when they risk it, they soon shut down, fearing reprisal in some way. The fear of consequences unconsciously controls the wavering person and is the central factor that makes a wavering person who they are. They are willing to put their toe in the water, but will soon run for safety. Their available-then-unavailable emotional state is like walking a tight rope with their partner, and when this is coupled with their lack of communication, it forms the typical portrait of the wavering person. This dynamic reflects their failure to directly address issues and reveals a pattern dating back to earlier childhood conditioning of negative reinforcement for having or feeling the way they do.

This seemed to be the situation with Bruce. He lacked the confidence to speak his mind and communicate with his wife. Whether his wife was truly demanding and angry was secondary to his own core issues. Bruce's fear of upsetting his wife and finding no other alternative but to leave was the crucial dynamic going on here. Once Bruce understood that, we were able to delve further into his earlier conditioning.

I asked Bruce to let me into his childhood world. He described vividly a mother who was a social butterfly – always buzzing from one activity to another and very opinionated. Whatever mother did, according to Bruce, she drove it into the ground. Nothing pleased her if it wasn't done right. Worse, her projects and thoughts were always present, constantly consuming the family's emotional space. Bruce felt that his mother didn't know the word "no," "not now," "later," or "can it wait?" His childhood was experienced as: "whatever mother wanted, she wanted it when she wanted it and in the way she wanted it."

In short, Bruce grew up with a sense that he was totally controlled and, worse, invisible to his mother. Whatever mother was involved in, everyone had to be involved in. Bruce's wants, needs, and opinions were constantly overlooked or put in second position to his mother's needs. As a result, Bruce eagerly sought to flee emotionally from his mother (and once, as I said, even to flee physically). In Bruce's eyes, escaping her presence became his only way to survive his feelings of engulfment, entrapment, and his sense that she always judged him as a failure.

I also needed to understand what role his wife, Rachel, played in all this in order to understand the dynamics being played out between the two of them. More often than not, people seek out a partner who fits their unresolved issues. What this means in this case is that Bruce was used to an assertive woman, not a passive one. On some level, he respected mother for her outgoing behavior. So, on the one hand, he was attracted to the positive side of his wife, but on the other hand, the same assertive behavior triggers a negative side in him. This is also why he floats between being loving to being detached from her.

When I met with Bruce and Rachel together, she did indeed complain that she couldn't feel safe in their marriage. While Bruce was sometimes very loving, she always had a sense that he was not truly there for her. She felt as if his bags were always packed and he was ready to go.

As you can see, Bruce's child was still in control of his life. Whenever something in his marriage bothered him, he resorted to feeling helpless and trapped, as if he had no say over what he would be "forced" to do or give up. That became his worldview as an adult.

My therapy with this couple focused on both spouses. For Bruce, we worked on understanding how the early messages from his mother continued to haunt him. By moving Bruce from his "child state" of feeling overpowered to his adult state of recognizing that he could speak his mind without fear of reprisal, Bruce could begin to take control over his impulses to leave rather than having his impulses control him. For Rachel, we worked on helping her be less demanding and controlling, as she too was a strong competent woman who wanted things done today, not tomorrow, just like Bruce's mother. As Bruce showed more emotional consistency, Rachel didn't feel abandoned and her raging behavior stopped.

THE "I'LL MARRY YOU WHEN..."PERSONALITY

The following situation is all too real for many women. They date the same guy for a long time and are waiting for the big question to be popped. The wait is even often reinforced by their partner's promise that when "X" happens – i.e. get a raise, pay off bills, take care of my obligations, etc – they can then commit to getting married. Unfortunately, the time gets extended and extended – and then it never happens. The woman is left wondering, was she just being used for sex, money, a fun time, or what? Did their potential partner really love them?

Situations like this are often indicative of a wavering personality. Often the issue is that one partner, usually the one who can't commit, holds onto a "flaw" that they see in their partner to justify holding back from marriage. And the irony is, this flaw is never so great that the person needs to wait to get married. Most often, the flaw is just a rational justification that the person uses to cover up an unconscious fear of commitment. And usually that fear of commitment centers around being controlled, trapped, confined, or committed. In almost every case, barring a scant number of legitimate ones, the individual's hesitancy is based on an early conditioning pattern where they were so controlled that the thought of being stuck means prison.

Meet Mark – a playboy par excellence. A successful professional with his own business, he had the wherewithal to buy, travel, eat, and play whenever and wherever he wanted. Over the years, Mark dated hundreds of women. But now, he came into therapy to discuss what his girlfriend called his fear of commitment. He admitted that he dated lots of women, but he always found some reason to let them go. But now he felt he didn't want to lose his girlfriend, so he agreed to show up in therapy for one session.

Of course, given my orientation, right from the start, I believed that Mark feared being controlled and that was why he couldn't commit. I began our first session by giving Mark the rundown on how I see relationships and that I wanted his permission to look into his past to see if there is anything that might support my contention. Mark agreed, and he began by describing his mother – a very powerful woman who at one time had been a nun. Mark reported that he has great respect for his mother, yet he felt that she was always in control of his life. He described his father as being passive and unavailable, because he worked long hours.

At this point, it was already clear that for Mark, a loving but controlling mother overpowered his little boy. Now as an adult he wasn't going to let that happen again. Through his work in therapy, Mark realized that he wanted to make a commitment to his girlfriend, and so he agreed that they would rent a house together to see how they would feel.

They had just moved in when I saw Mark one more time, after the following took place. Mark described that he was on the phone one day, and his girlfriend drove into their driveway honking her horn. Given that they had just moved in, she didn't have the remote garage door opener and so she needed his assistance to get into the house. Her honking had "made" Mark furious though, and so they came into therapy. Mark told me that he couldn't believe how selfish and unthinking she was to interrupt his important phone call just to have him go into the garage and open it for her. For Mark, that was all he needed. His little boy was just waiting for "mom" to show her true colors and overwhelm and control him. This scenario was all he needed to move out – and that was what he did.

It may not be the case that you are in a situation as tenuous as Mark's girlfriend. But if you are in a long-term situation where commitment just doesn't seem to be happening, I suggest you think in terms of Mark. Look and talk with your partner about the issue of control and how he or she experienced that in early life. Talk about how your behavior is perceived and whether or not your mate fears telling you how they really feel. By bringing the unconscious to the surface and discussing the root issues at play, it becomes much safer for a person to deal with this material and can bring the long awaited results you have hoped for.

THE "HARSH BUT NOT HARSH" PERSONALITY

We have been looking at cases in which a partner claims to want to be close, but unconsciously pushes attachment away out of fear of being controlled. Here is yet another pattern in how some people obtain distance from their mate, by pushing them away. I am referring to a segment of the population that uses harshness as a tool to find safety. In my experience, the harsh person occurs most often among women.

I have come to realize that many women are brought up to be the stereotypic female, sublimating their needs to a man. Let me clarify: it is not usually the parent's intention to make their daughter submissive, or to force her to acquiesce her needs to other family members, yet the conditioning is strong and clear. As a result, many women grow up feeling more powerless than they really are. I often see very strong women in my practice who are not in touch with their own strengths. It becomes an amazing contradiction within their actions. On the one hand, they are bright, competent, and educated and to the outside world they appear to be in charge. Internally, however, there are other dynamics at play. Internally, they often feel less than others, weak, or in some ways, inadequate.

Such women often enter therapy not knowing or not realizing how they talk, behave, or treat their loved one. They report having trouble in their marriage or relationship, but they often say their partner is loving, generous, and available and it is he who feels unloved, distant, and hurt. Meanwhile, the man reports that he doesn't understand why he is being treated the way he is, and that he feels used and unappreciated for the things he gives and does for his wife.

Consider Jane as an example of this type of woman. A 45-year old woman, Jane married her husband one year ago, when she came to see me. Jane reported that her husband was very unhappy with her behavior and he requested that they do therapy together to discuss why she treats him the way she does. We began talking, and Jane indicated that before they got married, she generally behaved herself, but now that they were married, she felt safe enough with her husband to let him know "what is on her mind." Now, I have no problems with anyone speaking up and sharing their thoughts, but what matters is how they do it. Often it is in the tone that they alienate their husband. Jane also admitted that, since they got married, she felt that she no longer has any breathing room away from her husband, but she always felt guilty when she told him no.

Jane told me that she never shared these feelings with her husband, so again, their communication suffered and did not support the couple in helping them find a way through their relationship difficulties.

As Jane and I explored her background, she reported that she was the only girl in a household of three brothers. She felt that her father favored the boys, and that much of the family time focused on her brothers' sport's activities. She also felt that there wasn't a lot of time for her and that even her mother enjoyed her brother's games and sporting events more than spending time with her. I asked if Jane had ever spoken up to her parents, directly asking for more attention, but she replied that she felt that the message from her parents was clear and so she never tried.

In effect, Jane felt that her needs became secondary to those of her brothers. As a child she felt no one listened. Of course, this set up a conditioning in Jane that continued to impact her as an adult. Today, her marriage some times brings up some of those same feelings. However, now, as an adult, she rebels, except she is rebelling with the wrong person. She cannot enjoy the wants and desires of her husband because she feels invaded and resentful. The only way for her to get her needs met now is to create distance from her husband by pushing him away. For Jane, harshness became her vehicle of choice. She became the "harsh but not harsh person" whose starting point is from a weak position, so she becomes aggressive and overpowers her partner to get her own needs met.

The resolution of this internal conflict for the harsh but not harsh person comes about when they begin to understand the core reasons for their behavior. They need to see that their reactions are stemming from unresolved issues centering around not being listened to, having to go along with the program, and sublimating wants. In order to feel safe, in control, and powerful, they must distance themselves to protect their wants.

What women like Jane need to do is to learn to communicate with their mate in a loving way. They need to inform their spouse when they feel pushed or controlled, and seek to discover new options that, as adults, they can take to create other choices and options. The key element to remember is that when the harsh but not harsh behavior surfaces, the person must realize that they have moved back into their child mode and must find more appropriate and loving avenues to address the powerlessness they feel.

THE LATCHKEY SYNDROME

The final case in this chapter concerns the type of person who experienced a "latchkey" childhood, by which I mean that the parents, siblings, and other caretakers were often too busy to give them any attention. When such people marry, their partner often reports an emotional absence.

Rose came to see me reporting that she was unhappy after eight years of marriage. She and her husband had no children, but she says they wanted it that way. Rose reported that she was happy with her life and that her time was spent working and playing tennis. She enjoyed many activities and looked forward to meeting her friends after work. She felt that she needed to constantly be active with her friends, and that her husband didn't have the same needs.

She described her husband as being bright, loving, and a homebody. She told me that he was plenty happy just to be around the house puttering or working in the garden, and that he was satisfied to wait for her return. But she also said that she knows he was unhappy. She believed her husband would never cheat on her, but Rose had a sense that she was not filling his wants. She therefore felt guilty, yet she really needed to do what she enjoys in her life. In seeing me, she wanted to know what to do to make their marriage work.

I could sense that Rose was a strong woman who knew what she wanted and went after it. I respected her strength and her desire to be active and social. But my hunch was that Rose didn't know how to stay true to herself and at the same time give in to her partner's wants of having her be part of his world. I wanted to know why she needed so much free time. Was it difficult for her to compromise her wants for his?

When I asked her this, she responded quickly with a resounding yes. She told me she loved her friends and needed to be with them, while her husband was content to just hang around the house. I could understand her point, but it was troubling that her behavior seemed unrelenting, in not giving her husband any time. Sometimes it is not what we want, but how much we want as well as the way we go about it that becomes the problem in relationships.

Rose agreed that her need for others was great, and in direct opposition to her husband whose needs were more for family and less for social activities. Rose told me that she didn't want to divorce over this issue, and so she was curious if she was wrong. There is no right or wrong to this issue, but each partner clearly had a different makeup. The question became, why was Rose so eager to be outside the home and was she willing to work on being less social and more at home? Would her husband be willing to work on being more social and less at home?

Rose didn't know if her husband would come into therapy, but she wanted to at least look at the part she played. She described her childhood. She came from a family where her parents worked 24/7 on their family business. She was an only child, so she spent a lot of time outdoors playing with friends. In fact, she relayed that her parents did not even require her to work in the family business, but that she was encouraged to leave the home to be with her friends. When I asked if she ever felt rejected because her parent's attention was directed elsewhere, she admitted that she did, but she also felt guilty because her parents just made ends meet. She simply felt that she couldn't ask for more of their time, because she saw how hard they worked so she believed that she needed to learn to entertain herself.

Now as an adult, it was clear that Rose was continuing on the same path of entertaining herself – and looking outside the family for comfort. Despite having a loving spouse who provided a home and wanted her presence, Rose didn't have a reference point and therefore she simply did not know what "availability" felt like. In her own life, she had never known it. To be asked to stick around now and to be the focus of someone's attention was literally foreign to her little girl. In fact, she even saw it as suffocating. She learned to not need anyone, and now she continued to not need.

Of course, it was also clear that Rose's husband had his own issues; why didn't he crave more socialization? But my focus was on Rose for the moment.

Of course, Rose could have remained single or chosen a less needy mate. Her choice of partner told me that on some unconscious level, Rose truly did want more for herself. On some level, she loved that her husband waited for her and needed her. Otherwise, she wouldn't have chosen this type of person. So she wavered. Rose wanted her husband, yet didn't know how to be touched or loved.

Learning about how her early years had influenced her today was key for Rose. She recognized that the conditioning of her past had taught her not to have emotional needs or to fear disappointment and rejection. She understood that she had married someone who was available and she admitted to herself that she truly wanted to be loved. Her therapy became to make this process conscious. When she was at home now, she worked on reminding herself that she could enjoy her husband's love and presence and that she wouldn't be pushed away.

THE RELATIONSHIP PARADOX

To conclude this chapter, let me remind you of the irony in many relationships. People typically become attracted to the very issue that triggers them. This is because they find it so easy and familiar to relate to that type of person.

But the irony is that the very dynamic we may be trying to escape from in our childhood becomes the very same dynamic that attracts us to a partner. Life is curious in this way. We seem to repeat patterns until we get it right.

But with awareness of your own dynamics, your life patterns

can be altered. The truth is, in general, people really don't want to detach from strong relationships they have formed, such as a marriage. All of us usually have an awareness that something inside drives us into behaviors that we know are wrong or hurtful. That is what brings so many people into therapy. On some level, they have an intuitive sense of how they contribute to the problem and they want to change rather than lose the person they love.

In summary, if your mate struggles with settling into the relationship, or committing to you, or vacillates between wanting you and pushing you away, loving then angry, think in terms of needing to find something from his or her past that made them feel a lack of control and a fear of repercussions. This is what drives them to pull you in and push you away. This is the wavering personality.

CHAPTER 6

OVERCOMING YOUR RELATIONSHIP CONFLICTS USING THE SELF-TALK METHOD

At this point in your reading, I am sure you have recognized your own behavior patterns and have decided if you are a dependent, wavering, or push-pull type of person. Perhaps you have also recognized which behavior pattern is typical of your current partner or a previous partner with whom you had a failed relationship.

If you have recognized yourself, let me congratulate you. Your willingness to do this soul searching and hard work will definitely pay off. As a therapist, I want you to know that you have already learned a tremendous amount about yourself, and about why you act the way you do. Just having this greater insight into yourself will really go a long way towards helping you improve all your relationships, not just your romantic ones. You can apply the knowledge of your personality type to any situation, be it with friends, colleagues at work, or even with strangers. You can now watch how you act and react with everyone you meet, and slowly come to better understand all your behaviors.

But there's more good news. I can actually show you how to change your behavior. If you are a push-pull person, I can show you how to recognize when you are acting out your tendencies to avoid or flee commitment. I can show how you can stay in situations and remain attached to a partner that you may truly want to love. If you are a dependent person, I can help you stop giving up your own needs so you can find healthy, loving relationships that make you feel good about yourself. If you are a wavering person, I can help you settle down into a stable state that allows you to make a loving commitment to a partner as well as to anyone else in your life.

Anyone can accomplish these steps to change. All it takes is a desire to take charge of your life as an adult, knowing that you don't need to continue the same patterns of behavior that you established as a child. You have other behavioral options available to you that can help you become and stay connected to those you love.

Let me be frank though. Change is not easy, nor can it be done in a day or even a few weeks. It takes time to become conscious of your behaviors and to take control over your thoughts and actions that you automatically perform day in and day out. These reflect patterns that you learned when you were very young, and so they reside deep in your unconscious. You resort to these behaviors because your unconscious mind knows no other way. Your childhood patterns are like a wound that continues to fester in your psyche.

My program can help you heal this wound. You can truly become aware of your negative behavior patterns and learn to catch yourself from automatically falling into them. My program is called the Self-Talk Method. I have developed it over the course of more than twenty- five years of counseling adults who are experiencing marital and relationship problems. What you will read in the rest of this chapter completely synthesizes the therapeutic work I do in person when I work with clients in my office. I am confident you can accomplish a great deal for yourself, just by reading this chapter thoroughly and practicing the Self-Talk Method on your own.

The Self-Talk Method is a 5-step process that begins with learning how to recognize when you are about to fall into an unconscious behavior pattern; and ends with learning how to expand your repertoire of feelings and actions so you can achieve positive outcomes with your partner – or with anyone. An overview of the steps is as follows:

❖ Step 1 – Identify that You Are Triggered

❖ Step 2 – Pinpoint the Trigger

❖ Step 3 – Remember that You Are Reliving Today's World from Your Child's Perspective

❖ Step 4 – Recognize that You Have Other Alternatives

❖ Step 5 – Choose a Healthy Resolution

Let me walk you through each of these steps in detail now. As you read, imagine yourself putting them into practice, and visualize how you can apply these steps in your marriage or relationship. I would like you to aim to first understand the concept, and then once you get it, you can apply the principles whenever you get triggered. Try to memorize the steps or take notes on them so you can do them even when you are in the midst of an argument or conflict with someone.

STEP 1. IDENTIFY THAT YOU ARE TRIGGERED

This book has shown you that your relationship or marriage problems boil down to issues of attachment and control that you carry from your childhood. The conscious and unconscious messages that your parents gave you about the degree to which you needed to stay attached to them and obey their wishes greatly shaped the development of your view of the world. Starting right when you were 18 months old, your unconscious mind was fed information about how much control you could exercise over your own destiny without risking the loss of your love object (your parents).

In the course of your early childhood, you absorbed these messages and developed a way of "being" in the world, that is, patterns of behavior that you applied to any situation to feel safe. You learned that it was either okay to be true to your Self or that it was not okay to assert your own needs. You received either approval or disapproval about being independent. You learned that you either had control of your wants or that others controlled you.

Growing up, the early behavior patterns and feelings about control and attachment that you learned as an infant took root in your developing mind. You began to interpret the world entirely from your inner child's perspective. As with all children, it seemed completely normal that you should behave in the ways you did. Your worldview became your personality. By the time you were a teenager, your unconscious mind locked in most of these thoughts and reactions.

So, if your parents made your young child feel smothered, it became automatic for you to prefer being independent and reject attachment or commitment to others. Furthermore, because of transference, your mind began interpreting many events and comments as if other people were trying to smother you. Whether it was your mother telling you to be home by 9:00 p.m., or a friend insisting that you go somewhere with him, or your high school sweetheart wanting you to date her exclusively, your unconscious mind tended to perceive many actions as seeking to control you. Whatever the situation, whenever you believed that someone was trying to dominate you, you automatically reacted by getting angry inside, closing down, and metaphorically or literally fleeing.

On the other hand, your child from the above situation might have responded by giving in rather than fleeing. In this case, your young child chose to feel or was made to feel dependent. You learned to stay attached to your parents and that you had no control over your true Self. It became entirely natural for you to abandon your needs in favor of others. Then, because of transference, you began to interpret many situations and comments as telling you to yield to others. Whether it was your mother forbidding you from riding your bicycle at night, or a friend insisting that you play a game his way, or a high school boyfriend never wanting to see the movies you wanted, your unconscious tended to interpret many events as forcing you to give up your needs. Whatever the situation, whenever you perceived someone who expressed their needs more strongly than you, you reacted by giving in, withdrawing, and forgetting your own desires.

In short, whether you were a push-pull, dependent, or wavering personality, the automatic behaviors that you developed in your early childhood now operate in your adulthood. You unconsciously perceive the world entirely from whichever perspective you established as a child. Whenever an event or comment does not suit your expectations of the world as you see it, you become perturbed, angry, upset, or just plain anxious.

In psychology, we call this "being triggered," in the sense that you are ready to go off. Some "cue," by which I mean something someone does or says, sparks your unconscious mind to re-experience the event as if you were a child again. Your mind interprets the situation as a threat to your sense of attachment and control, and you react with the same emotions you had as a child. If you are a push-puller, you probably feel angry and so you want to run away from the person who caused you to be upset. If you are a dependent type, you feel like giving in to the person responsible for your anger, even if you are not aware of that anger.

What you need to understand is that being triggered is your own making. It's your mind that perceives the cue as a threat to you. The fact is, the cue may or may not be threatening at all. Your partner, parent, sibling, friend, co-worker, boss, or stranger to whom you are talking may or may not be trying to hurt, insult, or control you. Even if they are, the point is, you are now an adult and you have many options available to you for how you might react and communicate with that person. You do not need to become triggered, which re-enters you into a childlike state and causes you to lose your adult rational mind.

The first step in the Self-Talk Method is therefore learning to recognize when you are triggered. This step is critical if you truly want to change your behavior and find loving relationships with others. This step is about becoming conscious of your unconscious and automatic behaviors. You can't make behavioral changes unless you become aware of your existing behaviors. It's that simple.

Fortunately, I assure you, it's easy to learn how to tell when you are about to become or have already become triggered. You can usually feel it in your body, because your mind sends chemical signals to your nerves and muscles whenever it becomes aroused by a perceived threat, even a small one. You've probably heard of the "fight or flight" response; that's what we are talking about here. Whenever we feel threatened, our body goes into the flight or flight response, with various neurochemical signals sent out from the brain to the muscles. Each person is a bit different in how their body reacts to the neurochemicals, but here is a list of the most common symptoms people experience when they are triggered:

❖ You feel adrenaline running through your veins.

❖ Your heart begins racing or you feel heart palpitations.

❖ You feel anxious, apprehensive, or upset for more than a few seconds.

❖ You feel like you need to yell, shout, raise your voice, be abrasive or sharp with the person you are dealing with.

❖ You suddenly develop a headache.

❖ Your muscles become tense.

❖ You feel fragile, ready to cry, or "out of sorts" with your normal emotional state.

❖ You feel like you don't want to talk or that you are closing down.

❖ You feel like you want to run away or hide from the situation.

These are all absolutely positive signs that you are about to become or were just triggered by an event or comment. What you need to remember though is that it is your unconscious child's mind that feels threatened, that believes the situation calls for reactive behavior. It is not your rationale adult mind that controls you at these times.

You now need to learn how to "reframe" your reaction so that it is more appropriate to how you, as an adult, can handle the situation with more consciousness, rather than resorting to your automatic, unconscious child behaviors.

Let's move on to Step 2.

STEP 2. PINPOINT THE TRIGGER

Once you've identified that you are triggered, you need to become fully conscious about it by figuring out what specific event or comment has triggered you.

In many cases, the trigger cue is obvious. Perhaps your spouse or partner said something that angered you and caused you to fly into a fury. Or perhaps you were expecting your spouse or mate to do something, and when he or she failed to do it, you took it as a betrayal of trust or confidence.

However, in some cases, pinpointing your trigger is much less obvious and detectable. You can't detect a specific comment or event that happened; you only have a subtle feeling inside that something is not right. For instance, you may have an intuitive sense that something is not going well with you or with your spouse or partner. There isn't a specific comment he or she said, but it feels like your relationship has deteriorated or become disconnected. When this occurs, it often seems like everything your partner says is wrong.

If you are in one of these ambiguous situations, try one of these solutions:

❖ If you are a push-puller, ask yourself the question, "Am I feeling afraid that I am being asked to give up my needs? If yes, what needs do I feel I am being asked to give up?" Asking yourself these questions can help you pinpoint your trigger because as a push-puller, you believe that something or someone is about to consume, control, dominate, or smother you.

❖ If you are the dependent personality, ask yourself, "Am I withdrawing or retreating because I am afraid that I will get into trouble when I have an interaction with my partner? If yes, what am I afraid of verbalizing to my partner? What am I trying to avoid telling him or her?" For you, asking yourself these questions might bring you closer to understanding your trigger because as a dependent person, you believe that you should not upset the apple cart with your mate, and you fear the collapse of your world.

❖ If you are a wavering person, ask yourself both sets of questions above to find out which side of the fence you may be riding at this moment.

STEP 3. REMEMBER THAT YOU ARE RELIVING TODAY'S WORLD FROM YOUR CHILD'S PERSPECTIVE

Being triggered literally sends you back into your unconscious childhood, where you felt threatened and afraid of losing some part of yourself. This momentary loss of your adult rationale mind is not under your control. As I said earlier, you are on automatic pilot, in a transference, when you're triggered, as your unconscious mind takes over your thinking and feelings. Whatever someone says or does, you experience it unconsciously from the same perspective as when you were a child being told what to do or how to feel.

If you are a push-pull person, being triggered makes you unconsciously re-experience your inner child who is being told what to do and asked to abandon your true self. If you are a dependent type, being triggered makes you unconsciously re-experience your inner child feelings of being small, worthless, and lacking or fearing the power to assert yourself.

Therefore, Step 3 reminds that you need to STOP, and get off of your automatic pilot. Recognize that you are seeing the world from your inner child. You are re-living an old script that reflects your inner child's feelings of being threatened, rather than living in the actual situation going on right here and now.

You therefore need to step back and see the situation more clearly. You need to remind yourself that your reaction has more to do with the helpless and powerless feelings that you once had when you were a child.

Here's an analogy to help you understand how important Step 3 is. Imagine a basketball player running down the court and suddenly realizing that he is going the wrong way. Unless he wants to make a basket for the other team, he needs to immediately stop, solidly plant his foot down, and pivot his entire body to change direction so he can head back to the correct basket.

Whenever you become triggered, you are like this lost basketball player. The minute your spouse's or mate's comment threatens you, or some event happens that bothers you, your unconscious mind takes over, confuses your rationale thinking, and makes you run the wrong way down the court.

An impulsive reaction is a key signal that you're going in the wrong direction. Depending on your personality type, you may be heading toward having an argument with your partner (or whomever you are dealing with), or you may be running away from them. Whichever goal post you are heading towards though, you are going in the wrong direction. Unless you turn around, your basket will be a score for the Conflict and Romantic Disharmony Team.

It doesn't do any good to do just Steps 1 and 2, identifying that you are triggered and knowing why you are triggered. You must do Step 3, which tells you to STOP and PIVOT to TURN AROUND. You don't need to continue going in the wrong direction. It is likely that no one is really threatening you, or that you have misinterpreted the situation. You are an adult, with many options open to you to resolve the conflict you are having with your spouse or mate. If you continue going in the wrong direction, you will certainly end up staying a victim in your child state.

If you can succeed in performing this critical Step 3, you will regain control of your rationale mind and truly learn to change your behavior for the better. Let's see how Steps 4 and 5 complete the process.

STEP 4. RECOGNIZE THAT YOU HAVE OTHER ALTERNATIVES

Step 4 is like crossing a river, from where you get on a new road and begin your real journey towards healthy relationships. In Step 4, you use your adult rationale mind to realize that you do not need to stay triggered about whatever happened because you have many other options available to you.

Your first option is to realize that you may not even need to feel threatened at all. It is possible that your spouse or partner never intended to control or hurt you. Whatever they said or did may have been completely innocent, or reflective of their own point of view, without any intention of controlling, insulting, dominating, or threatening you.

For example, you might recall from Chapter 4 the case of the woman who flew off the handle at her husband when he asked her what she wanted for dinner. In her mind, she believed she had firmly told her husband that she didn't want to cook, when in fact all that she had said was that she was tired from her day at work. Meanwhile, her husband believed his question was totally innocent, and said he was trying to assess what type of restaurant they might go to. An objective play-by-play analysis of this couple's conflict thus reveals that, beneath the surface, the husband was actually being loving and generous, while his wife's being triggered made her completely miss his kind gesture – and perhaps an opportunity for a romantic night out.

So, again, let me repeat the concept. Once you know you are triggered and have stopped and pivoted yourself, your first alternative choice is to re-evaluate your sense that you have been controlled or threatened. In all likelihood, you have not. You can calmly let go of all the symptoms that your body may be experiencing from your triggered state of mind. Relax. Breathe. Know your process and your patterns. Open yourself up to the many other options available to you as an adult.

By the way, even if your partner or anyone else is truly trying to control or threaten you, you will still benefit by considering alternative behaviors rather than staying in your triggered mode. Staying triggered clouds your thinking, and as I said, keeps you on automatic pilot, reliving your primal childhood fears rather than any real fears that might actually exist in your current situation. Unless you believe your life is truly being threatened, such as in a spousal abuse situation, you really will handle your situation better by relaxing and exploring both 1) alternative interpretations of what's going on and 2) alternative options that could help you resolve the conflict. Equally important is that you will experience the situation from a much healthier and less triggered perspective when you are in your adult mind than when you are in your child.

Once you relax and release to stop being triggered, your second action under Step 4 is to begin communicating with your spouse or mate (or whomever you are in conflict with). Communication with yourself and your partner is a fundamental key to finding other alternatives to resolve whatever conflict you are in. Communication involves many aspects of talking including:

❖ reviewing and clarifying what was said versus what was heard

❖ expressing your feelings about it (i.e., understanding that you need to speak from your adult, not your child)

❖ asking questions to understand the other person's real issues and staying more present with your own issues

❖ repeating information, to make sure that the two of you are having the same discussion, while staying aware of each other's process

❖ presenting ideas and alternatives with the awareness that this is not a win /lose game in which one of you wins and the other loses

❖ compromising, and

❖ selecting a final choice. ,

When you are triggered, you tend to think that you don't have any options and that you should continue arguing, or running away, or closing down. But if you can reach Step 5 of the Self-Talk Method, you will realize that you have many options to remain in the present situation and resolve whatever conflict you think you have with your spouse or partner. Step 5 reminds you to expand how you see things and remember that the consequences can never be as severe as you fear them to be. You can be true to yourself as well as to your love object.

Remember the two actions of Step 4: Relax (calm down) and Communicate – and you won't go wrong.

STEP 5. CHOOSE A HEALTHY RESOLUTION

Step 5 is the threshold for truly changing your automatic behaviors. If you've been able to recognize that you are triggered, that you are re-experiencing inappropriate fears from your unconscious inner child, that you have other options open and available to you, you can truly make progress towards choosing to have a healthy relationship. Step 5 adds a breath of fresh air into your life that allows you to stay in healthy communication with your partner as two adults who love and respect each other.

In practical terms, Step 5 involves having you – or you and your partner together – chose a way to bring mutually satisfactory closure to any conflict. In Step 4, you made progress by discussing, sharing your feelings, and being truthful about what bothers you. That leads naturally to Step 5, where you select some option that you can both agree to and happily live with. Your goal is to work out your feelings in a way that preserves your true Self, all the while also preserving your partner's true Self as well.

I am not suggesting that in Step 5, you should argue with your partner until you have gotten your way, or persuaded your partner that he or she is wrong. Throughout this book, I have suggested to you that relationships are always 50/50; no partner is ever right while the other is wrong. Each of you brings your own inner child's insecurities and fears to the table. Each of you is constantly acting out some hidden unconscious agenda for love, affection, and attachment. Each of you contributes to any conflict you have. And each of you must be satisfied with the way you come to closure over a conflict.

For example, the husband and wife who argued over dinner were each living out their own attachment and control issues. On one hand, the wife was re-enacting her sense of powerlessness that came from her childhood when she was not allowed to say no to her mother. On the other hand, her husband was acting out his own dependency on his wife, in that he believed that the solution should be to go out to dinner rather than take charge of the cooking himself.

In short, every relationship conflict has two sides to the story, and you both contribute a dynamic to causing the conflict. As a result, you both must be satisfied with the resolution and alternatives you choose in Step 5. You both must feel that you have been faithful to your true selves.

Resolutions to conflicts can focus on many options, but here are four to keep in mind in particular:

❖ One of you takes ownership for having made a mistake. This option can be a healthy choice, especially when it is done while you are not triggered. Admitting that you made a mistake actually allows you to remain true to yourself. Don't think of it as you being wrong while your partner is right, thus putting one of you below the other. The key to accepting this type of closure is to think of it as simply making a mistake of which you now take ownership. Even if you apologize and you don't feel you are wrong or giving in, but you consciously want to move forward without conflict, that too is okay.

❖ Both of you agree to disagree. This can be a healthy choice because the world is not black and white. Many conflicts simply reflect that you and your partner each want to have your own personal needs met. But as long as you communicate about it, and share your feelings, you can both feel good about this resolution.

❖ You generate new options together. This type of closure is usually very healthy, as the two of you end up working, even brainstorming, together to come up with a new option that is a far better choice than your earlier solutions based on the narrow perspectives you formerly had. I am sure you have done brainstorming before, such as at your work, and you know how powerful sharing ideas can be. In fact, brainstorming is an extremely effective method of generating good will and emotional energy within a couple.

❖ You understand your partner's dynamics and become more giving. Understanding your partner is just as important as understanding your own triggers. The more you can understand your partner's process (i.e., how he or she hears things and why), the more clearly you can see whether his or her responses are coming from their adult or their child. In fact, when you can see your partner's child, it means that you are out of your child and in your adult. To see the child in others empowers you. You can react with more understanding and without the sense of being threatened. You also become more giving and empathetic because you are no longer personalizing their reactions. You are able to go beyond the surface content of what is being said, to the core of what your partner really means.

Any of these four options can lead you to new behaviors that continuously reinforce your relationship.

Step 5 can be difficult. Many people find it truly frightening to give up their old patterns of behavior. They can go through Steps 1-4, then crash in Step 5 because they resort to blaming their partner for hurting or disagreeing with them, or they won't admit their own role in the conflict. But again, you have to continuously remind yourself that this is your unconscious mind reliving your old fears. If you are a push-pull person, you fear that you will lose your true self by compromising with your partner's desires. If you are dependent person, you are afraid of rocking the boat with your partner by asserting your true Self.

You need to get beneath your primal fear to successfully complete Step 5. Work with yourself to understand that what's at root in your fear is your unconscious belief that you have only two alternatives when it comes to dealing with others: that you will lose either yourself or your love object. Again, this fear derives from your early childhood when you believed that you would lose either yourself or the approval of your love object. This unconscious fear makes you think that both your options are lose/lose.

But as an adult, you need to understand that you have many more options for dealing with conflict with your loved one. You can decide to negotiate for a win/win. Whether you admit that you made a mistake, or agree to disagree, or brainstorm a new alternative with your partner, any of these choices can be win/win. Compromise shows that your adult is in control.

IMPLEMENTING THE SELF-TALK METHOD IN YOUR LIFE

It may take time to learn to use the Self-Talk Method whenever you find yourself in conflict with your spouse, partner, or anyone else in your life. But rest assured, when I work with my clients, they usually can walk themselves through the five steps within weeks of learning it. This is not to say that they are successful in performing the steps all the time, but they slowly and surely learn how to reduce conflict with their mate.

The Self-Talk Method teaches you to become conscious of how you love. You learn to catch yourself from reacting to your partner with the automatic defensive postures you developed in your early life. You learn to accept and take responsibility for your 50% of your relationship conflicts. And you learn to recognize that you have many options available to you to negotiate with your partner for healthy solutions that will keep your marriage or relationship intact.

Finally, remember that you can use the Self-Talk Method to work through any difficult situation or conflict you have in your life with anyone, such as at work, with your family, with friends, or anywhere. Anytime you find yourself becoming triggered, take it as a sign that one of your primal fears has been aroused, and that you need to walk yourself through the Self-Talk Method.

The Self-talk method will remind you of your entire emotional process in dealing with anyone. When you get upset, rather than reacting impulsively with an immediate automatic reaction, you can become aware that your attitude or mood has changed from the stable place you were formerly in, and that you are having a reaction that is more severe than appropriate. Then perform the five steps and you will see that it is entirely possible to negotiate any conflict to a satisfying, productive, and healthy closure that preserves your relationships with everyone.

EPILOGUE & SELF-JOURNAL

It is the deepest of human emotions to want to be close and feel safe with those who are most dear to us. That is why I have offered you this book, in an effort to help you explore two significant contributions to your personality that play a role in your ability to love and form a lasting relationship. Understanding your personality archetype -- whether you are push-pull, dependent, or wavering – and being able to identify your transferences will allow you to gain control over the triggers from your past rather than allowing your past to control you.

At this point, you have started to examine your relationship or marriage. If you feel unhappy or if your partner feels unhappy with you, let this book serve as a strong vehicle toward helping you attain the relationship you want. Make an effort to monitor your interactions with your partner. Little by little, using the analysis and tools in this book, you can learn to reduce the degree to which your past conditioning influences your ability today to form a healthy loving relationship and to stay connected to your partner for many years of happiness and fulfillment.

The remaining pages of this book are a Journal for you to use to reflect and write down notes about experiences in your life that relate to your separation-individuation. I invite you to review what you have learned in this book and jot down any experiences – positive or negative – that surface regarding the interactions you feel may have influenced your issues around intimacy and attachment. There are pages for you to note down your memories with your mother, father, and siblings/significant others at various times in your life, including your infancy, childhood, adolescence, early adulthood, and adulthood. There are also pages for you to write down notes about your attachment experiences in dating, being married, and even about the messages you may be imparting to your own children.

MY INFANCY SEPARATION MEMORIES WITH MY MOTHER

MY INFANCY SEPARATION MEMORIES WITH MY MOTHER
(CONTINUED)

MY INFANCY SEPARATION MEMORIES WITH MY FATHER

MY INFANCY SEPARATION MEMORIES WITH MY FATHER
(CONTINUED)

MY INFANCY SEPARATION MEMORIES WITH MY
SIBLINGS/OTHER SIGNIFICANT PEOPLE

MY INFANCY SEPARATION MEMORIES WITH MY SIBLINGS/OTHER SIGNIFICANT PEOPLE (CONTINUED)

MY CHILDHOOD SEPARATION MEMORIES WITH MY MOTHER

MY CHILDHOOD SEPARATION MEMORIES WITH MY MOTHER (CONTINUED)

MY CHILDHOOD SEPARATION MEMORIES WITH MY FATHER

MY CHILDHOOD SEPARATION MEMORIES WITH MY FATHER (CONTINUED)

MY CHILDHOOD SEPARATION MEMORIES WITH MY SIBLINGS AND OTHER SIGNIFICANT PEOPLE

MY CHILDHOOD SEPARATION MEMORIES WITH MY SIBLINGS AND OTHER SIGNIFICANT PEOPLE (CONTINUED)

MY ADOLESCENT SEPARATION MEMORIES WITH MY MOTHER

MY ADOLESCENT SEPARATION MEMORIES WITH MY MOTHER (CONTINUED)

MY ADOLESCENT SEPARATION MEMORIES WITH MY FATHER

MY ADOLESCENT SEPARATION MEMORIES WITH MY FATHER (CONTINUED)

MY ADOLESCENT SEPARATION MEMORIES WITH MY SIBLINGS AND OTHER SIGNIFICANT PEOPLE

MY ADOLESCENT SEPARATION MEMORIES WITH MY SIBLINGS AND OTHER SIGNIFICANT PEOPLE (CONTINUED)

MY EARLY ADULTHOOD SEPARATION MEMORIES
WITH MY MOTHER

MY EARLY ADULTHOOD SEPARATION MEMORIES
WITH MY MOTHER
(CONTINUED)

MY EARLY ADULTHOOD SEPARATION MEMORIES
WITH MY FATHER

MY EARLY ADULTHOOD SEPARATION MEMORIES
WITH MY FATHER
(CONTINUED)

MY EARLY ADULTHOOD SEPARATION MEMORIES WITH MY SIBLINGS AND OTHER SIGNIFICANT PEOPLE

MY EARLY ADULTHOOD SEPARATION MEMORIES WITH MY SIBLINGS AND OTHER SIGNIFICANT PEOPLE
(CONTINUED)

MY ADULTHOOD SEPARATION MEMORIES WITH MY MOTHER

MY ADULTHOOD SEPARATION MEMORIES WITH MY MOTHER
(CONTINUED)

MY ADULTHOOD SEPARATION MEMORIES WITH MY FATHER

MY ADULTHOOD SEPARATION MEMORIES WITH MY FATHER
(CONTINUED)

MY ADULTHOOD SEPARATION MEMORIES WITH MY SIBLINGS AND OTHER SIGNIFICANT PEOPLE

MY ADULTHOOD SEPARATION MEMORIES WITH MY SIBLINGS AND OTHER SIGNIFICANT PEOPLE (CONTINUED)

MY SEPARATION-ATTACHMENT MEMORIES WHILE DATING

MY SEPARATION-ATTACHMENT MEMORIES WHILE DATING
(CONTINUED)

MY SEPARATION-ATTACHMENT MEMORIES WITH
MY SPOUSE OR PARTNER

MY SEPARATION-ATTACHMENT MEMORIES WITH
MY SPOUSE OR PARTNER
(CONTINUED)

MESSAGES ABOUT SEPARATION AND ATTACHMENT
I MAY BE GIVING MY CHILDREN

MESSAGES ABOUT SEPARATION AND ATTACHMENT
I MAY BE GIVING MY CHILDREN
(CONTINUED)

If you would like to purchase my other book, *Why Love Stops, How Love Stays*, or to set up a therapy session with me, please contact me at 760-340-1114 in Palm Desert, California, or visit my website at www.drkreedman.com.